The Tibetan Art of Positive Thinking

The Tibetan Art of Positive Thinking

SKILFUL THOUGHT FOR SUCCESSFUL LIVING

CHRISTOPHER HANSARD

HODDER MOBIUS
Hodder & Stoughton

First published in Great Britain in 2003 by Hodder and Stoughton
Paperback edition first published in 2004 by Hodder & Stoughton
A division of Hodder Headline

A Mobius paperback

1 3 5 7 9 10 8 6 4 2

A CIP catalogue record for this title is available from the British Library

ISBN 0 340 82415 8

Typeset in Trump Mediaeval by Palimpsest Book Production Limited,
Polmont, Stirlingshire
Printed and bound in Great Britain by
Clays Ltd, St Ives plc

Hodder and Stoughton
A division of Hodder Headline
338 Euston Road
London NW1 3BH

This book is dedicated to those people who have discovered how thoughts create their world, and those people who are on the way to knowing this for themselves. It is also offered to the Northern Treasure School of the Tibetan Bon tradition.

On a personal note, this is lovingly dedicated to my wife, Silvia, and my daughter, Flavia.

CONTENTS

Acknowledgments

The writing of this book was made all the more easy by the sensitive, caring and detailed expertise of my editor, Caro Handley. Her talent and experience enabled me to speak in my own voice while keeping the ideas of the book accessible. Caro is a good example of the ideas expressed in this book. To my agent Kay McCauley, one of New York's finest and a constant guide, and of course my publisher Rowena Webb, who made everything possible.

Introduction

FIRE IN THE HEART

To the ancient Tibetan practitioners of the spiritual and religious discipline known as Bön, positive thinking was a skill to be learned and applied daily, in order to create a prosperous and fulfilled life.

Bön teaches that the skilful use of thought energy is the key to empowerment. To understand and transform the nature of our own thought energy creates what they call a 'fire in the heart'. This fire is the transformed essence of thought energy waiting for skilful use through our emotions, intentions and actions and with its power we can work daily miracles in our own lives.

The practitioners of Bön believed that its wisdom should be accessible to all. The principles they developed thousands of years ago are as valid and effective today as they were then. That is why I decided to write this book. Having been trained for twenty-seven years to know and understand the guiding wisdom of this great teaching, I wanted to pass on the knowledge which would help others to transform their lives.

Much of this knowledge is simple and straightforward. All of us, no matter who we are, where we live or what we do, can take the information in this book and use it in our lives to create positive change. The principles of Bön positive thinking can be applied to all the major areas of your life to bring clarity and insight, success, abundance and happiness.

Throughout the book I offer practical and simple exercises, based on ancient Bön rituals, which will help you to transform any area of your life. Though some of these may seem unusual or unfamiliar to those in the West, all of them are powerful and effective ways of bringing about change, both inside ourselves and in the world around us.

As you go through the book you will gain a deeper understanding of your thinking processes, the nature of skilful thought and how to use the 'fire in the heart' in your life every day. You will learn the immensity of your own thought energy and how to achieve the balance between gut reactions and intellectual thinking which will support all your actions and deeds.

The ancient Tibetans understood that the way you think affects everything you do. This is why by learning how to think skilfully you will be able to create new ways of living and to make your life emotionally and spiritually rich, as well as materially successful.

SO WHAT IS BÖN?

For 1200 years, until the invasion of Tibet by China in 1959, Buddhism was the dominant religion in Tibet. It is still the religion which most of the world associates with Tibet.

But long before Buddhism arrived there was another system of cultural and spiritual teaching in Tibet. Bön was a tradition that began 17,000 years ago and was predominant in Central Asia and Tibet for most of that time. The Bön teachings are less well known than the Buddhist teachings, but even in the ravaged Tibet of today there are thousands who practise Bön, and many other followers are spread around the world.

Buddhism supplanted Bön during a time of social unrest in Tibet and the two religions coexisted peacefully for some years. After a while, though, some Buddhists began to persecute Bön practitioners and so the Bön community, to prevent further bloodshed, took on some of the trappings of Buddhism. This developed into what is known as Reformed Bön, and its followers are known as Bön-pos.

The search for virtue, compassion and wisdom is the same for both Buddhists and Bön-pos; there is no major clash between them, and His Holiness the Dalai Lama has acknowledged the crucial and unique role of Bön in creating, defining and influencing Tibetan culture. Indeed, the fifth Dalai Lama once said that he was Buddhist by nature but Bön by heart.

Despite the emergence of the Bön-pos the original, undiluted Bön teachings remained very much alive and were known as the Bön of the Ngagpas. This is the tradition in which I have been trained. My teacher, Ürgyen Nam Chuk, was a Ngagpa, a person of high spiritual calibre. He was a tantric yoga expert and a lama, or religious teacher, as well as a physician of Bön medicine. He was also a shaman and magician. Not one of the Himalayan shamans who gained their status by being 'overcome' by the gods in a trance, but one who was trained in special knowledge and who was able to perform magic as a result. Men like him were the Merlins of Tibet, mystical, magical healers and masters of miracles.

The Ngagpas, who were identified by wearing their hair long, often in dreadlocks, looked after their communities. They performed birth rituals, weddings, funerals, divinations and rituals for the protection and benefit of the community, including control of the harvest and the weather. They also dispensed justice.

Ürgyen Nam Chuk came from the Nam or 'Sky' clan, which came from Lake Baikal in Siberia and settled in Tibet 1,000 years ago. However, long before this they had migrated regularly between Lake Baikal and Tibet and had become part of the Tibetan mythology and social structure.

The members of the Nam clan were famous for their medical skills, spiritual teachings and psychic powers and they had come to have great influence with the kings and tribal rulers of Central Asia and the Himalayas. Almost thirty years before the invasion of Tibet by China a senior member of the Nam clan foresaw the invasion and the clan, having warned the leaders in Tibet about what would happen, left the country. They settled in various Indian cities, adapting to aspects of Indian and Western culture.

In order to keep their teachings alive, some of the Ngagpas of the clan were chosen to travel to distant parts of the world, searching for those who could be trained to continue their wisdom and traditions. Under the practices of Bön, those of other races and cultures were not excluded from these teachings if they were spiritually and intellectually suitable. To find the chosen candidates the Ngagpas used a complex and profound astrological system which told them where in the world to go, as well as who they must look for.

One day, when I was four, my parents took me for a day at the beach. As the time to leave approached they called me to come. But I was reluctant to go. All day I had known that something important was going to happen, and that someone was coming whom I must meet. I watched the seagulls wheeling and the people gathering shellfish in the shallows and dragged my feet as my parents urged me to hurry.

'I have to stay to meet my teacher,' I told them.

As I trailed along towards the edge of the beach and on to the road I looked up and there he was. He laughed, and behind him a rainbow appeared. Ürgyen Nam Chuk introduced himself to my parents and explained that he represented a Tibetan spiritual and medical tradition which, using an astrological system, had suggested that I might be a candidate for its teachings.

My parents, not surprisingly, were taken aback. But they listened to Ürgyen and agreed to meet him again.

My parents were aware of the Tibetan beliefs about the reincarnation of spiritual teachers. But Ürgyen explained to them that he did not regard me as one of these but rather as a person with particular and special abilities, which related to medicine, healing and the spirituality of the Bön tradition. From his perspective I had a unique and rare consciousness which needed training. I was not to be regarded as perfect or special, nor would I be encouraged to think like this.

After several meetings my parents cautiously agreed to allow Ürgyen to teach me, providing it was what I wanted. First I had to go through a number of tests to determine whether the astrological process was correct and I was truly suitable. After this, Ürgyen began the teaching, which would continue for the next twenty-three years.

Although I was only four when we began, I was happy to be taught by him. His teaching was gentle, he made our lessons fun and I understood, deep inside, that this was what I was meant to be doing.

I went to an ordinary Western school, but before and after school each day and on weekends and holidays I would go to Ürgyen's house for my lessons. Ngagpas are free to marry and, indeed, to marry for love. Ürgyen's wife Tamdin was from a famous family of Buddhist teachers and the fact that Ürgyen and Tamdin were able to practise their religions side by side quite harmoniously for many years is confirmation of the common threads of Buddhism and Bön. Ürgyen had independent financial means, provided by his clan, and when he was not teaching me he gave free medical treatment to anyone who needed it and worked to help Tibetan refugees in other parts of the world.

I was, in most respects, an ordinary schoolboy. I played with my friends, sailed, climbed trees and scraped my knees. From time to time I got fed up with my lessons and decided to skip them. This never upset Ürgyen, who would wait patiently for me to return, which I always did.

All that Ürgyen taught me was by word of mouth. He never wrote anything down, he simply explained things to me, which I had to learn and repeat back to him. When I was very young he taught me simple principles and exercises. Later, after I passed puberty, he took me on to deeper paths of knowledge, all of them based on the power of skilful thinking.

He would test me on this knowledge with oral examinations, but he would also wait for me to experience physically what he taught me, so that I knew it with my mind and with my body. He taught me with kindness and compassion, never with anger or harsh discipline. The tradition he came from forbade the hitting of children, and he treated me with respect.

Central to what Ürgyen taught me were the Twelve Teachings of Bön, the very ancient and the earliest classification of Bön ever practised. In these Twelve Teachings you learn to gain spiritual balance and insight by working with the primal forces and thought energies of nature. Each of the Twelve Teachings, all based on the skilful use of thought and thought energy, is a means of transforming your inner and outer worlds, your mind, thoughts and consciousness.

These teachings, which can only be taught by a Master, lead the student to profound experiences of compassion and personal integration. Many more teachings followed from these twelve, and a further body of knowledge called the Gozhi Dzonga. Central to all these teachings was the principle of thought energy, in us and in the world surrounding us, and the great power for change, creativity and healing which this energy brings us.

When I was twenty-seven my education with Ürgyen was completed. He had taught me all that he needed me to know and soon afterwards he died. I was deeply saddened at his loss and carried out the rituals appropriate to the passing of a Master, on a consecrated place high on New Zealand's Pihanga Mountain.

When the rituals and blessings, which took forty-nine days and nights, were completed, I felt very alone, until I saw Jamma, the Loving Mother, dancing before me. She is one of the great Bön feminine deities of compassion and she transforms all types of obstructions and can guide an individual to deep states of mental development. As I watched her, all Ürgyen's teachings surged through me giving me strength and reminding me that I had become a Ngagpa.

My final act of farewell to Ürgyen was to place his drum into a special ritual fire, where it burned, covered in crushed juniper, a plant that has powerful purifying properties. As a great gust of wind suddenly sprang up to carry the essence of the drum away I saw my teacher flying on his drum around the sacred mountain of Bon-ri in south-eastern Tibet, paying his respects. Rainbows filled the sky and the sun and moon both cast their radiance on to the scene.

In Tibetan myth Ngagpas often flew through the air on their drums. I knew, when I saw this, that all would be well. I began to walk the long path down the mountain, turning back to pay my respects one last time.

I was free to do what I wished with the knowledge I had gained. Ürgyen laid down no rules and simply asked me to use my knowledge in the way that seemed right to me. For the next few years I travelled, practising Tibetan medicine and waiting for the right direction to appear.

Finally I came to Britain and established the Eden Medical Centre in London's King's Road, where I practise Tibetan medicine alongside a group of other skilled health practitioners, both orthodox and complementary, who have joined me over the years.

I was delighted to have created a healing centre to which people could come for their physical, spiritual and emotional care. But I felt there was something more I needed to do and so I began to write down the knowledge I had gained in my years of training, so that it could be used by anyone who wished to benefit from it.

My first book, *The Tibetan Art of Living*, was the result. In this book I explained how the wisdom and principles of Tibetan medicine can be applied by anyone in their daily lives, to improve their health, energy and wellbeing.

The Tibetan Art of Positive Thinking underpins every aspect of Bön teaching and belief. The use of Tibetan healing and medicine is reinforced by the use of positive thought energy. Use these ancient, effective and wise principles to bring about the change you wish for in yourself and in your life. The Tibetan art of positive thinking is a great force for good in the world, one that we can all understand, enjoy and share.

1
THE POWER OF THOUGHT

Every drop of rain that falls holds a thought within it ready to be woken from its dormant state. Every leaf that falls in winter or flower that buds in spring also holds the birth of countless thoughts. The infinite power of thought is in every creature, plant and object in the world around us. From the beating of our hearts at birth to our final breath in death, a continual stream of thought flows through us, making us, forming all our desires and directing unconscious actions, yet always guiding us towards greater self-knowledge.

The power of thought is immense. With simple effort and direction you can open your mind to an endless resource of thought energy. And having connection to this thought energy will open the way to a profound spiritual and material reality which will bring you financial, emotional and spiritual success. True thinking changes lives, yours and others.

Yet many people have no idea that this great resource is open to them. Often they feel helpless and seek meaning in the world outside themselves, without any awareness of the wonderful potential they have within. They don't realise that most of what they imagine to be their thoughts are nothing but the echoes of instinctive reactions to their environment and other people. There is a huge difference between the ineffectual, reactive 'thoughts', which can so easily occupy our minds for most of the time, and true original thought, which is filled with energy.

Your life is affected by unskilful thinking. Your future can be changed by casual thoughts or powerful emotions. By seeing and understanding what streams of thought flow through you and by taking control of your thinking, you will be able to start clearing away thoughts that hold you back or keep you suffering and choosing thoughts that will create happiness and wellbeing in your body, mind and life.

Knowing how to think creates huge personal power. It brings compassion to the way you see the world and awakens you to the thought energy in everything around you. It enables you to discover the deepest meaning of your life so that you can make it the life you truly want to live.

The ability to harness the power of thought was developed by the ancient Tibetan people in pre-Buddhist times. They had many of the same problems as you and me and through the Bön culture they discovered techniques with which to create a more fruitful and fulfilling life by transforming their thinking. This is part of a system called the Way of the Shen of the Cha and from it has developed the Tibetan art of positive thinking, a blend of practical wisdom and spiritual knowledge designed to increase happiness.

This art of positive thinking is alive and well across the world today and is still as effective as it was thousands of years ago. Through a series of simple meditations and exercises I will show you how to begin to experience and harness the great waves of thought that sweep through the world and how to use this energy for personal, material and spiritual empowerment. Through the power of skilful thinking you will be able to remove negative thought patterns, transform your emotions and develop effective, life-changing ways of thinking.

* * *

'You are what you think.'

My teacher's words hung in the evening air. We sat together high on Mount Pihanga, in the centre of New Zealand's North Island, looking down at Lake Rotoponamu, as the winter sky turned from bronze to black around us.

'Thought directs all things,' he said. 'People pride themselves on how they think, but really it is thought that moves through people. Our thoughts create our lives, they make us sick, happy or successful. Our thoughts can pollute our planet through the actions we take. Thoughts on their own will gather like clouds in the sky, good thoughts coming together with other good thoughts and unskilful thoughts attracting other unskilful thoughts.'

I listened to his words with care. For years I had been learning about the Bön way of thought development, and how to use thought energy to heal, protect and overcome obstacles. That afternoon I was preparing for an ancient Bön ritual of rebirth. I was fourteen years old and felt excited that he considered me ready for the ritual, but I was also apprehensive about what I would have to do.

I was placed in a hole several feet under the ground, with a tube to breathe through and the earth was replaced above me. Buried alive, I remained in darkness for twelve hours while my teacher performed special ceremonies to transform my mind and body.

As I lay, cold and still in the darkness, I saw and confronted the nature of my own negativity. In those twelve hours my mind and body went through a kind of death. In this state I experienced the shadows and radiance, good and evil, the corrupt and the inspirational aspects of my human nature – all stemming from the energy of thought. And as I confronted my negative thoughts, within them all shone a light, clear, unstained and pure.

From deep within me I felt the power of thought and the power of life. For there, buried with the worms, going through this ancient Bön ceremony, I discovered that true thought creates and remakes every part of us, second by second, and that our bodies and personalities are just the wrappings to a consciousness far more profound.

After he had dug me out of my grave, my teacher sprinkled me with a mixture of Tibetan beer, water and milk and brushed me with branches of juniper. As I sat next to him, exhausted and cold, I felt and saw a great plume of dark smoke rise from within me and enter the clear burning ceremonial fire he had lit in front of us. Ürgyen had psychically directed my old consciousness into the fire. I had gained a new life. A life where thought in all its magnitude flowed through me. Where I could start to connect consciously to all life and participate in it.

The mountain upon which I now sat, the lake and the other great mountains nearby all sang a deep droning song of the earth's powerful undercurrent of thought energy.

'You can hear it now, that's good,' whispered my teacher, and with that he went to sleep.

I gazed out at the landscape, and there within the mountain range I felt the thought energy pulsing, as though the great mountains themselves were nothing more than waves of rock being tossed up by a great ocean. From the small town nearby I felt the thoughts of its inhabitants, floating like the smell of cooked food on a Sunday afternoon. Some were loving, pleasant and happy, others were sad, despairing, jealous and angry. All had different sounds and smells; every one of them had a history of a life wanting to be better. So one by one I listened to them all and sent them healing and the power to overcome difficulties. As I finished, the stars were gathering over the mountaintops and the air was heavy and chilled.

'Everyone wants a better life, it starts in the heart and ends there also.'

Ürgyen's words filled the silence. His body was asleep but his thoughts were wide awake. Suddenly everything folded in within itself and all that was left was one continuous pulse of thought. Then came a brilliant light and then silence.

The silence filled my heart and as I looked out over the land I knew that the entire world is a thought and that we all are thoughts within it.

What I learned on the mountain that night long ago, in that profound and ancient Tibetan ritual, changed my understanding of the nature of thinking for ever and created in me a longing to pass on to others the things I had learned. Please don't try such a ritual, because it requires a specially trained Master to perform it safely. Through performing the exercises and meditations I will outline, you will be able to reach a deep understanding of thought energy in a similar way.

NEGATIVE THOUGHTS

The first step to harnessing thought energy is to understand the power of negative thoughts and to learn how to banish them.

No one on this earth is alone. We only become alone or lonely if we believe, at an unconscious level, that we are separated from the thought energy of the earth and the many people it connects us to. This belief of separation is fertile ground for negative thoughts. It can begin in the womb. Pregnancy is a great expression of thought and its energy in the material world. We can pick up negative thoughts as we grow in the womb, and those very first thoughts can influence our behaviour throughout our lives.

If you constantly think in a negative way you will shorten your lifespan. Relationships become fearful and problems increase. You lose your ability to discover joy in simple things. This creates further negativity. Life becomes complicated. Negativity adores all things that are overly complicated. Complication conceals negativity, keeping it safe from exposure. You get so caught up in the complications that you lose sight of the underlying negativity that is creating the problems.

The Twenty-Eight-Day Removal of Obstacles

This exercise can be used for any kind of obstacle or problem and works very effectively. It removes patterns of negative thinking and replaces them with strong, positive thoughts.

Do the exercise morning and evening, always at the same time. Sit comfortably either in a chair or on the floor. Take at least twenty-five minutes for the exercise and carry on for longer if you wish.

Mornings are the best times to start and Thursday, regarded as a day of prosperity, is the best day on which to begin, according to Bön beliefs for the overcoming of obstacles. You would finish on a Wednesday, which is a day of action. You must continue for twenty-eight days because this length of time helps to develop mental energy to a level of power and intensity that will create effective change.

Start each session by focusing your mind on your problem or obstacle. As you focus on it think of it being burned away by fire, or smashed to pieces by a large hammer. As it is destroyed, the negative thoughts behind the problem will be revealed. Don't search for them, just allow them to surface as you focus on smashing or burning your problem.

As you continue to do this all your negative thoughts towards your problem will be purified, creating sudden and powerful bursts of positive thought energy which will solve your problem and heal the situation.

When you have finished, sit in silence, giving thanks for the hardships of the past and the good things this practice will create in the future.

Remember, the world, you, your mind are all built on thoughts. The more you do this practice the stronger your ability to create change will be and the stronger your mind will become. But always allow at least seven days of rest before beginning the twenty-eight-day exercise again. This gives time for change to become evident.

Louis was a musician who never got the financial rewards he deserved for the work he had done. He wrote music and lyrics for well-known bands and singers, yet he was hardly ever paid or given any recognition. With children to feed, rent to pay and a marriage in crisis due to financial pressures, he was desperate.

When Louis came to me for help I taught him how to discard all his negativity, bad luck and how to create positive energy and good luck by doing the twenty-eight-day practice of focusing on overcoming an obstacle. So for twenty-eight days Louis sat each morning and evening focusing on one thought, the destruction of his negativity, and the creation of vitality that would attract all the money he was owed and create opportunities for the future.

Soon after the twenty-eight days ended Louis's life began to change. Money flowed in from past efforts, people began to think of him for projects and he established a presence.

He went from being a nobody in the minds of others to a person worthy of respect as people acknowledged that he had written successful songs and was very talented.

Louis still does this twenty-eight-day practice whenever he wants clarity or insight into a situation, or to solve problems as they arise. His sense of helplessness has gone and has been replaced by a strong sense of his own worth and ability.

In ancient times and during the reigns of the Dalai Lamas, Tibet was a violent place. It was common for spiritual teachers to have thought wars, especially if they were asked to defend one kingdom against another. The people of Tibet were warlike, despite their spirituality and religious influence. While armies fought, these people would send thought missiles at each other, often killing people, causing defeat or making enemies give up the desire for war. The ability to know how to use thought energy was an important survival skill regardless of a person's station in life. The stronger your thought energy, the greater your vitality and thus the greater your potential for spiritual growth.

In the same way psychic and spiritual healing, often from a great distance, would take place. Just as these great masters of the past could do this, there are people today who also have such skills.

Through my teacher I once witnessed the practical application of this great power of thought energy in the most astonishing way. 'Thoughts can kill, create, heal and protect,' my teacher had taught me. A few days later we were in a small town in New Zealand where we saw a man and a woman arguing. The man started to become violent and was hitting the woman. From where he was sitting, a short distance away, my teacher projected the thought energy of non-violence and stopped the man in his tracks.

The man turned in astonishment, having found himself unable to continue being violent. He knew my teacher had done this but had no idea how and didn't know what to do. As he stood there he became scared of his own violence and then he felt the fear and pain he had caused in the woman, and she experienced his rage.

They came over to Ürgyen and asked what had happened. He told them how thoughts of any type bind people together and how violent thoughts create violent actions which in turn damage lives and emotional and mental balance. The couple told us they had experienced a feeling of peace, calmness and a desire to stop fighting. Having experienced one another's suffering they found a more skilful way of communicating and learned to love each other more kindly. Ürgyen had used thought energy in a gentle way to stop them from hurting each other.

I too have used thought energy once in this way, to stop an extremely violent situation. I saw a man draw a knife in a jealous rage, as his girlfriend stood talking to a friend. I knew that he was in danger of harming her, or someone else, so I used the power of thought energy to prevent him. Astonished, he dropped the knife, unable to understand why he suddenly felt his violent urge disappear.

Thought energy should only be used in this way in exceptional situations where you can sense that it will be of benefit. It is not good to interfere in other people's lives unless absolutely necessary in order to prevent harm.

To begin to understand the art of Tibetan positive thinking we must first look at our emotions and how they influence the way we think. The ancient Tibetans believed that the majority of people only react through emotions or desires even though they may think that they do not. So true thought, and therefore control and direction of your life, can only start when you discover the origins and learn the lessons of your emotions and desires.

THE NATURE OF EMOTIONS

Happiness for most people is the result or outcome of a course of action, which in turn has come from a desire of some type. This desire is a thought, for all desires and emotions are a form of thought. Desires and emotions have different levels of intensity or duration, like wind or waves, or light in the morning or evening. Both leave traces of energy behind them after they have gone.

Each emotion or desire leaves a mark or effect within you, and by learning how to identify them you can then mentally gather them up in a ball of string and start tying them up, so that like horses pulling a chariot they can be of use to you. Each of these marks contains essential information about every experience you've ever had, what you learned from it and what you ignored. Knowing how to use and harmonise these emotional traces is the start of knowing about the power of thought.

HOW TO DISCOVER THE ORIGINS OF YOUR EMOTIONS

Sit comfortably. Then stretch your body as best you can. Close your eyes. Focus your mind upon your physical heart. Imagine your heart starting to soften and release emotional energy. At first lots of emotions may come to your attention. As they do, identify with the ones that are most intense, and then summon them to you. Name each emotion, then give thanks for it.

After you have done this, offer up this emotion in exchange for a more beneficial energy, a transforming one, or a thought energy that can move an obstacle. For instance, you might exchange grief for acceptance or understanding, or you might exchange resentment for humility or laughter. You are ransoming the origins of your emotions for the energy of insight.

The idea of ransoming emotions for energy is an ancient Bön concept and is safe, very helpful and immediate in its effects. The concept of ransoming is easily understood if you recognise that we make choices and trade off one experience for another many times each day. By choosing to ransom emotions for energy you can do this with more discretion. The more you do this, the more clearly the origins of your emotions are revealed and the stronger your insight becomes. Ransoming your emotions humbles your ego, enabling it to stand aside as you gain self-knowledge.

At the heart of each emotion that is ransomed you will find love and humour. Why? Because every human being is naturally born with the ability to love and to laugh. So don't be surprised if you end up laughing at yourself and loving yourself a little more.

It was night and the waters of Lake Rotoponamu lapped around my feet. Two months had passed since the burial ritual. The water was growing stiller as Ürgyen started to awaken the lake's natural powers. Lakes according to Bön hold information about the land around them, as water stores energy. All lakes hold history and the thoughts of those who pass by. A lake can be used as a window to gaze into the mind of the world. As we both stood there, the wind dropped away, the sky darkened and the lake became dead calm. Ürgyen started to sing to the lake, using sacred sound to awaken the thought energy within the lake. As I looked at it, the lake changed and did indeed become a window on the world.

There was a tap on my shoulder. One of the Maori Elders who gave my teacher permission to use the lake and mountain to help train me smiled and said to me, 'What can you see?'

'I can see everything!' I told him.

My teacher and the Elder laughed and left me to gaze into the thoughts of the planet. First came the distant past, then the present, then the many futures open to humanity. At times I was in tears. Then I gazed upon myself, as the lake and I became the same. I awoke to find myself floating in silver water, and through a haze I saw my teacher and his Maori friend gazing at me. It was as if a curtain were drawn across a divide between the world I was in and the world they occupied.

All my thoughts started to take on shapes and identities, some pleasant, some frightening and I felt that I was dying yet again. The lake had become universal thought energy, the planet earth some distant island. Rivers of souls rushed past me, like comets on the way to rebirth, and I was being transported into a new existence by the thought energy I was contained in.

A hand reached through the curtain and pulled me, as if through a membrane, back on to the shore. I saw the stars, but this time they were no longer distant points of cold light: every one of them had an identity, a voice, each one was a thought in action following its own course.

Suddenly strong instant coffee was poured into my throat and sweet potato stuffed into my mouth. 'Don't gaze on the universe with an empty stomach,' the Maori Elder said, confirming what I had already discovered, that it is impossible to concentrate fully when you are hungry.

My teacher grunted in agreement.

Lake Rotoponamu looked at me.

I looked back.

I still carry this lake with me wherever I go, for all lakes and mountains are one and the same and teach us the enduring nature of thought and its energy.

THOUGHT POLLUTION

Have you ever had the experience of walking into a room and feeling uncomfortable or overwhelmed, or the feeling that you know a place intimately even though you have never been there before? This is because your underlying thought energy is picking up all the other thoughts that have accumulated there in the past. Such thoughts are similar to dirt and grime that have built up in a kitchen that has never been cleaned. Before we can know all things and become empowered we must start by preventing ourselves from being influenced by the unwanted thought energies of others. In the atmosphere around all of us is a lot of thought pollution.

Thought pollution results from the unskilful use of emotions, the most basic element of thought energy. Often when we feel down or sick it is because we are picking up these thought pollutions, which we can absorb very easily. But we can also learn quite simply how to remove them from our minds and bodies and to extract the positive thought energies they hold.

There are eight common thought pollutions which, according to the ancient Bön teachings, affect us all. They are:

- Envy
- Jealousy
- Greed
- Anger

- Lust
- Arrogance
- Careless actions and thoughts
- Selfishness

Bön teaching suggests that if we experience these thought pollutions in a very intense way they can affect the way our brain functions and lead to varying degrees of depression which influences our physical, emotional and spiritual health.

Spirituality is directly connected to our brain's ability to function and the way it communicates with our body. So spiritual ill health can lead to physical ill health. The brain and body are catalysts of highly developed thought energy. So it is important to develop pathways of energy between the brain and body so that thought can flow between both and both will be inspired and empowered. These pathways are created by directing thought energy from your mind through your body and out into the world.

The eight thought pollutions carve out pathways between the brain and body which are not beneficial. These pathways can create suffering, misfortune and emotional and physical illness. In order to find the origins of any mental or physical illness, or run of misfortune that we have experienced we should look at these thought pollutions. If you can identify the emotional force behind anything negative that is going on in your life then you can change it. Remember, though, that the emotions are the teachers of human experience and we must always give thanks for them. They must not be denied but understood, loved and transformed.

Emotional energy is the starting point for learning how to think, because emotions are the blueprints of the fundamental urges of humanity. We are all emotional beings, but some emotions govern us more than others and these emotions can pollute us internally if we allow the unskilful use of them to become habitual. In truth, we all do this every day, in big or small ways. We incorporate such energies into our ways of living and they then become pollutions, obscuring our potential for clarity, thought and success.

According to Tibetan Bön wisdom the eight categories of thought pollutions apply to all of us, and of these certain ones will influence each of us more than others. These pollutions are regarded as mental toxic waste, generated by emotions that are unskilfully applied.

Outlined below is a description of each of the eight, the effect they have upon us and the characteristics they engender in us. Use them to discover which thought pollutions influence you most and which emotional type you are. It is important to note that there is no sense of wrongdoing to be associated with these thought pollutions, as there is from the Western religious point of view. You should feel no guilt about them. They simply occur through ignorance and a lack of understanding about the nature of thought. So be kind to yourself as you explore them, but at the same time be as honest as you can in order to reap the maximum benefits.

At the end of each description is a mental exercise which can help you transform each particular pollution into positive thought energy. Use the exercises for the emotions that influence you most, in order to clear the thought pollution, remove its negative influence from your life and transform it into positive energy. These exercises may seem simple, yet they are profound and powerful and will clear emotional blockages which may have held you back for many years. Unless stated there is no specific length of time for the thought exercises. Simply do each for as long as it takes.

THE EIGHT POLLUTIONS

Envy

Envy can lurk behind smiles, promises, friendship and many other human interactions. It limits happiness and causes illness both in the person who is envious and inthe person against whom the envy is directed. When you are feeling envy you lose your sense of joy and connection to others. Envy is not productive and creates unhappiness.

People who are dominated by this emotion find it difficult to take advice or to learn from their mistakes.

Thought Exercise to Transform Envy

Sit down and make yourself comfortable. Imagine yourself washing your face, hands and head. As you clean yourself with fresh water, your heart becomes lighter. The water takes on the impurities of envy, turning it a dark muddy brown. As you finish washing, your heart is open and free of envy. At this point you gaze into the muddy water that has accumulated in a bronze bowl. As you peer into it, you start to see images and situations that come from your envy. You start to gaze upon the nature of your past envy and the damage it caused to you and others. As you do this, take responsibility for each situation you witness and then let it go.

Jealousy

Jealousy is not like envy, which is calculating and brooding. Jealousy is a moment of passionate, untamed, raw desire that someone has something, whatever it may be, that you do not. Being jealous is like having temporary blindness, because you can only see the object of your jealousy and the world seems shrouded in semi-darkness.

Thought Exercise to Transform Jealousy

Though simple, this meditation is very effective. Sit by yourself in a quiet place. Out loud – very loud – ask your inner self to show you your jealousy both in your daily and inner life in every detail. Accost your jealousy by shouting at it to go away.

Give thanks for this.

Greed

Greed plans an assault, because greed is tactical. Greed is not just for food, or wealth but also for ambition, power and even happiness. It is an unskilful emotion that seeks to accumulate anything in order to feel safe and secure. Greed creates ill health and problems with insecurity, money and relationships. Greed is like the erosion of land by the sea or wind, invisible but real and very destructive all the same.

Thought Exercise to Transform Greed

Go to a place of natural beauty, near the sea or water and close your eyes. Listen to the wind, the sea or the sounds of running water. Focus on one of these sounds so that nothing else enters your mind. Now direct this sound to start eroding your greed and replacing it with an appreciation of the natural order of things and an understanding that all things come to fruition in their own time.

Anger

Anger comes into being when a person is overwhelmed by the world and feels powerless to change it. This sense of powerlessness grows in intensity and creates anger which becomes part of an individual's reactions to the world, both externally and internally. Anger is unskilful self-recognition, a burst of intense energy that creates a sense of awareness.

People influenced by anger seek perfection in all things and see themselves as leaders and inspirers of other people. Anger creates an imperfect experience of divinity within such people, who are otherwise spiritually perceptive.

Thought Exercise to Transform Anger

To transform anger first think of how you can be of service to your fellow human beings. Think about why your anger takes place in the way it does. Focus upon your thought energy to bring you a greater experience of love and spirituality in your daily life.

Lust

Lust just wants to make everything okay. Lust is the need for control over the world and the personality. Lust seeks to identify everything by its own experience; it does not believe in anything but its own actions. Lust and arrogance are related, like the two ugly sisters in the story of Cinderella.

People influenced by lust seek the company of others and tend to value community and human relations. People matter to them more than anything else, but at the same time they try to make themselves the centre of any human interaction.

Thought Exercise to Transform Lust

Sit quietly. Listen to others without offering your opinion or projecting your personality. You do not have to make others in your image. Experience the wisdom and beauty of others and in turn they will discover yours.

Arrogance

Arrogance is lack of confidence. Arrogance is unsure about what to do, so creates a defence system of emotions. Arrogance sits at the heart of all the emotions listed here. Arrogance would like not to be arrogant but is too afraid to stop; it doesn't know how to change.

People influenced by arrogance believe that things don't last and that they can only rely upon themselves. They often seem apart from others because they lack skills in creating friendships.

Thought Exercise to Transform Arrogance

Sit quietly. Consider what you have achieved. What is its real value? Are you happy? Do you know anything about yourself? Do others know anything about you? Do you share yourself with others? Do you have any real friends? Consider these questions with absolute seriousness. Then as you gain insights, cultivate them with self-love so that you will be able to recognise opportunities for positive change.

Careless Actions and Thoughts

Careless actions and thoughts are emotional and material events which are spontaneously thoughtless and careless and which then have long-lasting effects and repercussions, for instance being spiteful, hurting another person or passing on gossip. Careless actions and thoughts can often come about when we are strongly influenced by the other emotional pollutions.

People influenced by this emotional energy have not yet learned how to tap in to their stillness and make use of their emotional resources and can be careless and clumsy in thought and action.

Thought Exercise to Transform Careless Actions and Thoughts

Spend thirty minutes first thing every morning doing this meditation. Sit in a chair, arms in your lap. Focus your attention on your day. See your day becoming a faultless event in which you control each outcome with harmony and balance.

Selfishness

Selfishness comes about when an individual has no self-awareness either physically or emotionally. This lack of self-awareness leads to loneliness, which in turn affects the chemistry of the brain and the body's limbic system, both of which are intimately connected to our emotions.

Selfishness becomes addictive. The more a person experiences it the more they are prone to becoming dependent upon the energy of selfishness. Being selfish steals your vitality and leaves very little time and energy for anything else.

Thought Exercise to Transform Selfishness

Lie down on your back with your arms and legs stretched out comfortably. Imagine your body starting to dissolve and slowly turning to ash. All that is left is your physical heart, beating, and your mind, which inhabits your heart. From this point, your mind starts to regenerate new thoughts which create new emotions, which create in turn a new more complete physical body free from selfishness.

So, now that you have understood the role and importance of your emotions, and the thought pollutions that can impede your development of skilful thought, it is time to look more closely at the way thought energy can be used to create happiness.

THOUGHT ENERGY AND HAPPINESS

Every person on this planet is linked by their thoughts to every other person. Each one of us can use thought energy to create happiness. True happiness is a balance of thought energies, woven together so that they support each other and create harmony.

You have a right to this happiness as long as you share it. This is true of money, wealth and spiritual achievement. If you do not share these you cannot hold on to them for long, or you will end up damaging your ability to think and feel. We have the right to own things but not to abuse ownership. We should own our inner achievements and share those achievements with others, but we should never give away the thought energy behind our achievements. This energy is sacred to each of us and is unique once developed.

Thinking in a positive manner in the Tibetan way simplifies all things, and naturally creates happiness, success and love. The more love you can create within yourself the more useful your thinking becomes. Thinking well means taking control of your life. That can be a scary thing to do, because it means taking responsibility for the way your life turns out. We are not subject to some greater force that dictates our every move. As individuals we can determine the outcome of each moment and thus the main events in our lives, by paying attention to the detail in order to direct the outcome.

THINKING SUCCESS INTO REALITY

Establishing three ground rules can create success of any type. These are:

1. What you want should be for your ultimate good and benefit.

2. You must be able to carry the creation of what you want through to completion.

3. You must decide how, once your aim is achieved, you will apply it, what you will do with it and how achieving it will change you.

Success is not an ultimate conclusion in itself but the result of a series of steps made possible by creative thought. Success comes about through thinking it into action. Once you are comfortable with each of the three ground rules, you must think about success of whatever type you want to the exclusion of all else. You need a time frame. Give yourself a calendar year as the time in which to achieve your success. You need belief in your ambition and not to fear the possibility of failure. Your life must change in order to be successful.

In other chapters you will learn specific techniques to apply to achieve success in specific areas of your life. But this general approach is the basic foundation to activate the dormant power of your positive thought energy.

DEALING WITH DIFFICULT PEOPLE

One of the major obstacles on your path to success is likely to be difficult people. We all encounter them and the difficult situations they create in life. So before we go any further, let me explain how to use the power of positive thought energy to help you to deal with such people and situations.

How do you define what a difficult person is? The Tibetan Bön tradition describes it in this way: A difficult person is someone who throws their emotional energy at you, causing you upset and shock and making you feel defenceless. A difficult person is someone who persecutes you or obstructs your path in life. A difficult person is someone who tries to cause you emotional or physical harm or damage your reputation. A difficult person is someone who tries to steal your belongings, wealth or creativity.

Such people can be easy to deal with, but the golden rule is that you should not at any juncture wish them harm. What you must wish them is self-knowledge. You can direct the thought energy of self-knowledge to them in such a way that they will lose their sting towards you. Do this exercise twice a day, in the morning and evening.

Sit quietly focusing upon the individual and picturing them in your mind. Then direct this thought towards them, speaking it out loud either three or nine times:

'May all blessings flow to you. May self-knowledge flow to you. I reclaim the power you have taken from me, it is mine to take back, it is my right.

May love and good fortune come to you now. As I speak now you are no longer a problem for me! Your difficult energy dissolves into wisdom. You regard me with respect.'

At the end of this clap your hands three times very loudly to seal your invocation.

This exercise works with great effect. Think of this as a spiritual kick in the backside that leaves no bruise, creates no harm and gives you a compassionate view of the situation and the difficult person or people concerned. Compassion cannot be derided or made small, for it is the biggest force in the mind of humanity.

Jenny was a teacher, whose career and life were almost destroyed by a woman at her school. This woman was a senior teacher and was also Jenny's boss. She decided for no obvious reason to make Jenny's life intolerable and for two years Jenny suffered humiliation, extra workloads and accusations of dishonesty. Although Jenny was found innocent of the accusations the head teacher did nothing about her tormentor. This woman then began to telephone Jenny at home and verbally abuse her.

At this point Jenny was seeing me for a physical condition. One day she broke down in tears, telling me of her dreadful situation. I showed her how to use her thought energy as in the exercise above and Jenny went away delighted that there was something she could do herself about the situation.

To Jenny's astonishment, within hours of her starting this exercise the head teacher suddenly decided to act on Jenny's behalf and dismissed her persecutor. Free of the woman's damaging behaviour Jenny was able to continue happily with her teaching career.

Two years later, Jenny was at a conference when another young teacher told her how he was being bullied by his boss. To Jenny's surprise it turned out to be the same woman, who had simply moved on to torment someone else. Jenny taught him the 'dealing with difficult people' exercise and heard later that the woman had been banned from teaching permanently.

TURNING NEGATIVE SITUATIONS INTO POSITIVE ONES

As you go through life, using skilful thought to create success in your life you will, at times, need to change a negative situation into a positive one in order to move forward.

To do this it takes the power of strong, positive thought energy. So how do you start to identify the negativity of a situation and its potential for change? You need to do the following three things:

1. Identify the cause of the negative situation and how long it has been going on.

2. Look at the way people concerned with the negative situation react to it, how much negative energy they invest in it and whether they believe it can change.

3. Look at what the possible outcome will be if the negative situation is changed into a positive one and whether, once changed, it will last and become stronger.

Once you have done these three things, honestly and with care, you will find the raw material for change. This is what you do with it:

Sit quietly. Imagine a fire is burning in front of you and that you place sweet-smelling oils on to the fire. Then take what you have discovered the raw material of the negative situation to be and cast it on to the flames. There you see it begin to melt and as it melts, with the power of your thought and the heat of the fire, you mentally direct it to become positive, pleasant, powerful and beneficial. As the situation changes the fire changes too; the orange flames become a brilliant blue-white column of light. This column then moves into your body and into your spine, then flows into your brain and your heart. From within you it flows out into the world, broadcasting the powerful and positive thought energy that will change the negative situation into a positive one.

You will get results immediately after using this exercise.

Lydia and Ian were a young couple who had met in my clinic. They were very much in love and wanted to see the world. So they decided to travel and get to know each other better as they did so.

In a certain Asian country, as they were about to leave it on a flight home, they were arrested by local police and charged with not paying their hotel bill. This was wrong but they had no choice and went to jail, separately, terrified for themselves and each other. Thankfully, before their trip I had taught them certain skills in case they got into trouble. The exercise for turning negative situations positive was one of them.

Having a strong mental link with each other, they did this meditation on their own and for each other. Forty-eight hours later they were both released without explanation, their passports returned with their luggage. However they found that all their money was gone, as were their tickets. So they sat down in the busy street and did the meditation again. At this point two elderly tourists offered them a lift to the airport in their taxi. When they arrived at the airport, this elderly couple guessed something was up and Lydia and Ian told them the whole story. The couple paid for their tickets home.

Lydia and Ian took their address and when they returned home they sent them the money.

When Lydia told the story to her uncle she discovered that her uncle knew the elderly couple and had not seen them for ten years.

There was a debt repaid and a very happy reunion.

A THOUGHT FOR THE DAY

Each day we wake in the morning with a thought in our minds. This thought, whatever it may be, sets the tone for the rest of the day. This is not always a good thing as we may wake up in a rush for work or school, with a hangover, feeling depressed or generally in a state of confusion. Therefore it is a good idea to learn how to create an original thought to begin each day, and to make the day a perfect expression of your original thought.

What do you want from each day? Do you want peace, career and financial success? Perhaps you want the end to a personal issue. Whatever you want, you have the power to create it, as long as you know what to do with it. Here is how you can start to empower your daily living through releasing creative and dynamic thought energy.

Begin each day by giving thanks for the simple fact that you start each day with endless opportunities for change. As you start to be thankful you will notice that you gain a heightened sense of intuition and that this makes you more aware of how your thought energies affect your daily life and of the sense of fun and wisdom behind each habit. As you understand why you have the habits that you do, you will start to sense the energy of original thought.

This process can take place in just seven days, and then you will be able to discover what you need most each day to be fulfilled. You can then focus on that in the morning and direct it to happen during the day.

Tibetan teachings suggest that in order to gain a strong ability to make each day all that you want it to be you must train your ability to direct thought energy using the following exercise.

Choose all that are relevant to you from the list of thoughts below and then focus on each one for three days at a time, beginning first thing in the morning.

A day of peace
A day of good relations with everyone you come into contact with
A day of tangible success in your career that is recognised by those in power
A day of attracting tangible wealth to yourself
A day of enhancing your reputation
A day when you meet a person that you can love and be loved in return
A day when you can overcome domestic problems of any type
A day when you recover from sickness
A day when you gain independence from any negative influence
A day to find a new house or accommodation
A day to find a new job or create a new career
A day when powerful people bestow favours and good fortune upon you

A day for [illegible]nd problem solving
A day to c[illegible] or those who seek to harm your rep[illegible]
A day to r[illegible]
A day to t[illegible]
A day to c[illegible]

If there is a[illegible]ou need to focus on which is not already [illegible] then you can include it in your list.

Say each th[illegible]ke this: 'Today I will make this day a day [illegible] is a day when I will attract tangible wealt[illegible]at the thought in this way eighteen time[illegible]be silent for a few minutes as you see th[illegible]t spread out into your day, creating the [illegible]t you have just invoked. Speaking each[illegible] with strong intention, is the easiest way to [illegible] of your thought energy. This invocation wi[illegible]nection to the endless power of thought en[illegible]

You can rep[illegible]oughts in this way as many times as you [illegible]

When John's [illegible] brain tumour he was left to care for their [illegible]d daughter. He had no relatives who c[illegible] knew so little about the domestic side[illegible]fe that he couldn't even boil an egg or iro[illegible]had taken care of everything while he wo[illegible]iness.

Soon after his wife's death John lost his job and had to default on his mortgage. The bank was less than sympathetic and foreclosed on him. It seemed that everything had gone wrong for John. With a child to care for he needed to find a job and new home very quickly. Yet job after job interview came and went.

Desperate to change the tide of events John came to me and I taught him how to direct his thought energy towards solving his problems and finding the home and job he needed. John practised the exercise faithfully for some days, until eventually he went for a job interview which seemed to go well.

At the end of the interview the owner of a small oil and exploration company asked him about his current situation. It all came tumbling out and John thought he had blown it.

'I understand,' said the owner. 'I've been there, I know what it's like. Oh and by the way you've got the job and you can use the company apartment until you get settled.'

That was five years ago. John went on to become chief executive officer and close friends with the generous and compassionate owner of the company.

The power of thought is everywhere, in all things. Unseen but very real, it creates the reality that we know and experience. By learning how to harness and use the Tibetan art of positive thinking you can start to create the reality that you want and to make your thoughts direct successful actions and outcomes. Merely to react to events in your life will always leave you feeling that you are tossed and pushed around by life. By connecting to the thought energy of all things then you choose to work with life, to be in charge, rather than to be powerless.

Choose this path and your life takes on new dimensions of meaning, success and happiness. Life works in partnership with the higher dimensions of your consciousness. You start naturally to celebrate life and life celebrates you. Remember that all material things are thought energy in action, just as you are pure thought in action. Allow the power of thought to flow through you and begin to harness pure thought energy, using the skilful application of your will and mental intention. In this way your thinking becomes a communication with the divine within you and a direct and powerful tool for influencing the material world.

In the following chapters I will show you how to develop and use skilful thought energy in order to create benefits and success in specific areas of your life: your work, finances, health and wellbeing, your sense of personal freedom and your relationships with family, friends and partners.

I will also show you how to help and encourage others, both those you know and strangers, so that the blessings of positive thought energy can be shared and passed on. Finally, I will show you how to travel further along the path of spiritual enlightenment and how to develop your consciousness so that you can connect, at the deepest level, with the unity of all things and the single thought which links every one of us.

2

THE NINE KEY MOMENTS IN LIFE

Our lives are enormous. We live in busy, demanding and hectic times in which each day merges into the next and it's easy to lose track of the quality, the meaning and the sense of purpose that give life its significance. Too often we live life feeling tired, drained or in a race to keep up with all there is to do. Yet every life can be a celebration and a great opportunity for success, spiritual benefit and skilful thinking.

Tibetan Bön belief suggests that we have nine key moments in our lives. Each one is a marker that defines not only which direction our lives may take, but also what we need to learn at that point in time. These nine key moments happen over and over again, in many different forms. Sometimes they last a second, at other times they last for months, as we go through a major experience. Often we are overwhelmed and don't know what to do or what is happening to us. Yet full awareness of our key moments is vital if we wish to live vibrant, transformative and exciting lives. If key moments pass you by in the blur of daily life or in the overwhelm of the moment then you miss wonderful opportunities for growth and for the development of skilful thinking and the chance to learn from and direct your own life.

In this chapter I will outline the nine key moments, so that you will begin to recognise them as they happen in your own life. As you come to experience each key moment you will become aware of the thought energy behind the moment, and how you can use this to create blessings and happiness. For each key moment I have included a thought exercise to develop this aspect of your life more deeply. All nine exercises are useful and valuable, but you may find that particular ones feel relevant and important to you and that you wish to try these first. Trust your instinct about which to follow, or work through all nine, one after the other.

The exercises are simple, and I have included examples, for each one, of people who have successfully used them to make changes in their lives. These stories make change sound easy – and it is. Using these exercises it is quite possible to make major changes to your life in a short space of time, provided you are willing to be open to change and to stick with the exercise. Often we put off dealing with painful issues in our lives, afraid that trying to change will be too hard and too complex. Yet change need not be difficult or complex, for the most profound and important things in life are always very simple.

The nine key moments that every person has in life are:

Birth
Family
Love
Success and failure
Meaning
Happiness
Acceptance
Independence
Death

Each of these nine can happen at any time in your life. From each there are vital things that you need to learn in order to understand how the experience affects your thinking.

Sometimes key moments appear in our lives as problems. As with all types of problems, we often make them more complicated than they need to be. A problem appears to teach us a simple lesson and this is normally to be found in the nature of the problem itself. By developing skilful thinking we are able to see the true meaning of why things happen and to see the value in our problems far more clearly.

If they are fully experienced and understood the nine key moments will act as bridges to move us into a more mature state of thought and spiritual evolution. So let us now explore each of these nine key moments one by one.

BIRTH

It happens to us all and it surrounds us all the time. Living creatures, people, animals and birds are being born everywhere.

According to the Bön view you were already one year old when you were born, with many thoughts, feelings, aspirations and concerns already formed, though you could not yet express them. The ancient Tibetans used the lunar calendar, which was shorter than ours and which contained many changes and monthly variations, and this is why they believed a newborn child was one year, and not nine months old.

From the moment of conception and throughout your time in the womb you started to learn how to think, and thought energy began to influence your development and health and to create the underlying patterns for your future life. The way you were born indicates the way you see life. This means the nature of your mother's labour – whether it was easy or complicated – as well as the nature of your mother's thoughts and your father's emotional state, from conception until you were born.

But birth is about far more than just the act of being born. Birth is a powerful thought energy that is with you all the time, unfolding into a continually developing physical, emotional and spiritual experience. It exists in the way you think, in the opportunities that life gives you and in the way you respond to them. In fact, we are all in a state of birth continually and the other eight key moments arise from this first one.

It is possible to discover the meaning of birth in many different ways. It may be an actual birth or it may be a creative or personal breakthrough, the birth of a thought, an idea, a state of mind or a decision. Of course birth is not always positive; there may be the birth of a problem or difficulty in life. But even at the worst of times there is an opportunity to be found in birth.

Think about moments in your life when you have experienced birth in all its forms: a child, a golden opportunity, love, friendship, a stroke of good luck, a sudden understanding or a new phase or beginning in your life.

The Birth Thought Exercise

This is a wonderful exercise for everyone to do, but especially those who feel old, depressed, jaded or tired of life and those who wish to be more open. It's also very useful for improving communication in a relationship, if you or your partner find it hard to open up to one another. Ideally you should both do it.

Do the exercise each morning, for at least ten minutes.

Have ready a blank exercise book you can write in and keep as a birth book.

Sit in whatever way is comfortable to you. Close your eyes. In your mind's eye, see a soft white light. It forms slowly into a beautiful white egg. It grows larger and larger until it surrounds you. Soon you feel that you are in the centre of the glorious white and pure egg. You feel renewed, a sense of rejuvenation flows through you. You feel yourself becoming younger, day by day, hour by hour, minute by minute, until all that is left is your thought energy just as it was in the first few hours of your conception. In this special place, you can see all of human life and experience.

All of mankind passes by you; from your quiet place you can see and hear the hum and rattle of humanity. Then within the egg a soft red light begins to pulse and it grabs your attention. You follow this light, and the light takes you through your time in the womb, through each day of your life within your mother, through your birth, then through each day until the present.

As you relive your days something important happens: you begin to know the birth energy in each day. You start to feel the vitality, the opportunities taken and missed, the sad, bad, good and excellent moments of your life, all revealing the birth within each of them. You know then why your life is the way it is and you understand that you have the power to change it. At this moment, breathe in through your nose and blow gently out through your mouth.

Rest for a few minutes. Then write down what your experience of this exercise was like and what emerged as most important for you in your birth book.

As you continue to do this exercise each morning you'll find that all kinds of realisations and discoveries, born from the exercise, will appear in your mind through the rest of the day and night. Note these down in your birth book. This exercise will reveal the beauty and power of birth to you. As you continue to do it all your routines and habits will become imbued with thought energy, enabling you to think more clearly. You will start to connect with the deepest and most profound parts of your consciousness and to feel reborn. You will become an explorer and you will search for and find the true meaning of your life. In learning how to recognise the key moment of birth, your life will take on new depth, meaning and quality.

All her life Marcia felt she was struggling, yet she didn't know why. At the age of eighty-four she felt clueless about the nature of this struggle and bereft of happiness. Marcia had children, grandchildren and a husband who loved her, yet she felt that there was a barrier between her and the world. She had felt the presence of this barrier since childhood. Marcia felt she was on a desert island, unable to feel emotions fully.

When I first met Marcia she was not one for conversation, so I didn't try to talk to her, I just told her how to do the exercise and said that she could practise with me, if that helped.

She started to do it every day, and after a few weeks she started to talk.

Marcia told me that she had been over-protected all her life, first by her parents and then by her husband. She had been a pretty child, like a little doll, and it was as though she had been kept in a protective box by her parents. Then, when she grew up, she picked a husband who treated her in the same way, keeping her 'safe' and tucked away from life. Marcia spent her life feeling removed from all that was going on because this was precisely how she lived.

'I did not know what life was,' she told me. 'I thought it

was the things I did, not the things I am. I started to realise that although the things I did influenced me and changed me, they were not the real me. I have hidden behind my family and I did not know anything about the fundamentals of life.

'Now I know that everything now has a life of its own. I have discovered my self and I am happy with that. I have discovered the ability to seize every opportunity and to love my family far more than I ever thought possible. My husband and I have become reborn in our relationship.'

Marcia taught this exercise to her husband and adult children. She shared her discoveries with them, and all her worries and emotional garbage fell away. She started to look and feel younger, she built bridges and she discovered the full heights and depths of emotion by discovering birth in all its guises.

FAMILY

We all search for family, for a sense of belonging and joining together with others. Our birth family is our first experience of community; the family we were born into gives us the view of family that we take out into the world, where we often create new families with partners, friends or colleagues. Family gives us a sense of belonging to the world and influences the way in which we think. If we allow ourselves to be included in the thought energy of family, which is everywhere in our daily lives and experiences, we enrich all our relationships instantly. We can share the thought energy of family with anyone we interact with, whether it's a chat with a stranger, an exchange with a shop assistant or a meeting with work colleagues.

In everyday life many people close themselves off from

others, diminishing their interaction, and reducing their quality of thought. Many opportunities to experience the power of family pass us by when we are closed in this way. Opening up to family thought energy brings people together and cuts through prejudice. It creates a feeling of goodness, sharing and togetherness. It teaches us the value of people in their own right – not for what they can do for us or for what they have, but for what they are.

The key moment of family happens when we feel love in all its forms. It can be sexual love, romantic love, spiritual love, platonic love, the love of friends or acts of kindness from strangers. In each key moment when we feel consciously connected to the human family lies one of the greatest spiritual and life-giving experiences we can have. These moments happen all the time, but too often we are not conscious of them. Instead we are caught up in the thought energy of routine, habit and unskilful thinking patterns.

We are each other's family, and you can experience this by becoming aware of the key moments of family in your life, with all the gifts this will bring you.

THE FAMILY THOUGHT EXERCISE

This exercise is excellent for those who feel alone, separate from others or disconnected from their own thoughts and feelings. It is also excellent for anyone who has family problems, who wants a family or for those who have been adopted and wish to find their birth parents. Use it also if you are on the brink of divorce, if you have problems with colleagues at work or between friends who live together.

Do this exercise in the evening for about ten minutes before bedtime.

Sit quietly and as comfortably as you can. Close your eyes and in your mind feel the top of your head. Move down, mentally, to your face, shoulders, arms, fingers, chest, belly, hips, legs and feet. Then feel the rise and fall of your breath, in and out like an ancient wind, blowing the collective wisdom of the family of mankind.

Listen. Try to hear what is in this wind, which is your breath and the breath of others. The air that you breathe has the key moment of family within it. Begin to sense the needs of others and the desire for community, for belonging to a family unit. Feel this as you link your breathing with that of everyone else.

Now extend thoughts of wellbeing towards all others and send the energy of healing, comfort and communication.

When you finish give thanks for your day and for all the people you have met throughout the day. Then, as you sleep, direct your deepest thoughts towards learning from the thoughts of others, so that when you wake you will be a little wiser and more open than you were before.

Paul was the odd one out in his family. He was not like the others in his family or other children in the street where he grew up. He wanted to know why things were as they were and how things worked. Paul's parents couldn't understand him and so he felt rejected by them.

Although Paul wanted to love his family he felt separate from them and this began to influence his whole life. Paul didn't know how to make friends or how to have intimate relationships. He was deeply unhappy and very lonely.

As he did the family exercise, Paul began to see how and why his family did not know what to do with him. Because of this he forgave them and started to understand how they saw him. To his amazement he discovered that they were in awe of him.

With his new awareness Paul was able to build a loving relationship with his parents, brother and two sisters. He has made new friends and no longer feels separate from others. In fact, people often come to him for advice on relationships.

LOVE

Love is everywhere but is difficult to pin down, it can be hard to experience and more complex to share. Love is the unspoken language of consciousness that makes sense of the majority of the world that we unconsciously occupy. By learning how to understand the thought energy of love your consciousness expands and your life becomes more creative and fulfilled. Although love thought energy is not academic it can create great intellectual achievement. Love seeks us out and presents itself many times in many guises. It is the one key moment that constantly offers itself to us, but because we are normally unaware of its presence in our lives we do not notice it. There are great streams of love energy moving through our planet and so there are opportunities to receive love all the time, if you open yourself to receiving it.

The thought energy of love will liberate you, show you your own value, bring you harmony and balance and show you the endless joy that exists in human consciousness. So how do we become aware of this key moment in our lives? We invite it, as we would an old friend or someone we wish to get to know better.

THE LOVE THOUGHT EXERCISE

Use this exercise if you feel unloved or unloving or in any way out of balance. It is valuable for those who feel joyless and bound to duty. Also for those who believe they have found the perfect love and for those who are about to get married, as well as for those who have a problem in a love relationship, such as lack of passion. The love thought exercise will reveal both the positive and the negative sides of a love relationship and will help you to discover what the relationship needs.

Do the exercise for ten minutes a day on waking.

Sit down and be comfortable as you can. Place your thoughts and concentration into your physical heart. Let your attention be completely focused on your heart to the exclusion of all else. Think of your heart as a reservoir from which endless blessings can flow. Feel your heart beat and let each beat reverberate through you. As this happens feel the energy of love between your heartbeats. In the deepest parts of your body, mind and soul, the thought energy of love exists, waiting to be acknowledged by you. As you feel this thought energy of love in your heart, invite it to flow into your mind, body, life and thoughts.

Doing this exercise regularly will start you on the path of transforming your life. The recognition and acceptance of the thought energy of love will give your life extra dimensions and greater richness. You will heal and enrich your love relationships and you will feel abundant and see abundance in your life, because the experience of love is abundance.

Maria was a successful academic, very distinguished in her chosen field and the author of many highly acclaimed books. Her talent had brought her a comfortable lifestyle, but Maria felt a deep discontent underpinning everything else in her life, because she felt so unloved. For ten years she had shared her life with Mark, another very successful academic. Theirs was a very cerebral and dry relationship. They appreciated one another's talents and gave each other a lot of support in their chosen careers, but there was no passion.

When Maria came to see me she told me that she didn't know whether she loved Mark or not. She liked and admired him, but felt there should be more than that. She did not feel loved by him, or appreciated for her femininity. He always put work before her and the two of them had never discussed marriage or children. She felt he would be happy to go on as they were, but she wanted something more.

I asked Maria to do the love thought exercise every morning for a month and just to see what came up for her. When she came back to see me she was excited. After two weeks of doing the exercise she had decided to talk honestly to Mark about her feelings, her hopes and dreams. To her surprise he had been very moved by what she said and had told her that he too would love to marry and have children.

Maria and Mark had got stuck, both presuming how the other one felt, instead of communicating openly. After they talked Mark too began to do the love thought exercise. Two weeks later they talked again and decided to take a romantic holiday together and plan their future.

The exercise had put both of them in touch with the loving and romantic sides of themselves and given them permission to open up. With this great energy shift Maria discovered that Mark could be a surprisingly passionate man. He began bringing her flowers and writing her love notes and she not only felt loved, but discovered a depth of passion in herself which matched Mark's.

Two years on Maria and Mark were married and expecting their first child. Both had put their academic careers second to each other and to family life and both were extremely happy.

SUCCESS AND FAILURE

Success and failure always go together. One brings the other, they are the same thing, and this is why they come together as a key moment. Many people see success as the achievement of a goal or aim, while failure, we are led to believe, is bad or at least unfortunate. But in the Bön view these definitions are too simple. True success is there to lead you to be compassionate towards other people. Failure takes place when you forget this. Both success and failure are vital ingredients to help you cultivate wisdom and insight.

The world is full of successful failures: people who see themselves as successful, but whose success is hollow and worthless because it is based on dishonesty and does not benefit others. Sometimes huge companies collapse in a spectacular way; this is because they are based on dishonesty. They see themselves as invincible, but they are not.

It follows that success can be unfortunate and failure the best thing that ever happened to you, because from failure we learn how truly to succeed, in a way that will benefit us as well as others.

The material world demands that success and failure come together, as a means to regulate the limited life force of our delicate planet and our fragile species: humankind. The key moments of success and failure teach us the true meaning and value of actions, thoughts and deeds. They show us our responsibilities in the material world, through our morality, our ethics, our work and the way we deal with other people.

We have a tendency to measure our success by how much pleasure it brings and failure by how much pain. This approach comes from a lack of connection to the thought energy of success and failure. Once we connect to this thought energy and see why we have success and failure in our lives we start to see that neither success nor failure is as clear-cut as we imagined. A success can be a failure, a failure can become our greatest success.

As you shape your future your attitudes to success and failure will determine your achievements and the path you will take for yourself. Knowing that success and failure belong together you will never again be taken in by either. Instead you will be wise enough to know that one will always be followed by the other, and both will have great value in your life.

THE SUCCESS AND FAILURE THOUGHT EXERCISE

This exercise is useful if you are facing any kind of success or failure in your life. Coming to terms with big life changes, such as the end of a relationship, the loss of a job or a serious illness, can often involve feelings of failure. This exercise will help you to see the other side of the experience and to understand that where failure is present, success is there too.

You can also use this exercise if you are going through changes or if you wish for success in a venture. The exercise will help you to see whether you are on the right path, whether the venture is right for you, and if it is right it will help you to reach a successful outcome.

Do this exercise for at least ten minutes, morning or evening.

Sit quietly and close your eyes. Think of the times in your life when you have experienced successes and failures, great and small. Think about how they have affected you, spiritually, emotionally, mentally and in your material circumstances. Once you have done this try to feel all the thought energy associated with the successes and failures you've had. Feel them as deeply as you can, then direct them to flow like warm gold water, drop by drop, into your heart. As you do this, you will gain the essence of each of your failures and successes and this will bring you self-knowledge. As you finish the meditation give thanks aloud for every success and failure you have had, naming them as you do.

If you have a particular venture to focus on, then visualise it before you finish the exercise. Be as specific as you can about the subject matter and your intention. You will get a strong feeling about whether it is right for you or not and what the outcome will be.

Jane wanted to buy a house. She had looked at dozens and she had set her heart on a particular one, a spacious and beautiful house in a good area. Jane's husband wasn't worried about which house they moved into; he left the choice to Jane.

The price Jane offered was accepted, but then the problems began. First she and her husband couldn't sell the house they lived in, then the seller put up the price of the house they wanted by a large amount. Jane was determined to have the house, so she sold their home for less than it was worth and agreed to the higher price for the new house.

Still more problems arose. The survey showed that the house had all kinds of problems which would cost a lot to repair. Jane's husband suggested at this stage that they give up and find another house to buy. But Jane wanted this house. She had taken her older sister, whose opinion she relied on heavily, to see it and her sister had loved it. So Jane pushed ahead with the purchase. At last the house was bought and Jane and her family moved in. But from the moment they arrived the family had troubles. The children became ill, Jane and her husband began fighting, the neighbours were awful and the repairs to the house cost more than they could afford.

It took two years for Jane to accept that this house was never right for them. At this stage I suggested she did the success and failure exercise. Through doing the exercise she realised that she had been guided by her sister's judgement, not her own. So she sold the house to her sister, who loved it and had no problems there.

Jane used the exercise to decide whether to go ahead with the next house she found. This purchase was a success and she and her family moved into a home that was trouble-free and lived there very happily.

MEANING

People create pain in their lives when they lose track of or cannot find the meaning in their daily activities. Absence of meaning can be like a void and creates a sense that all we do is futile.

Many people try to find meaning in their lives through the eyes of others. They look for approval, reactions and information that will tell them who they are. But this can only result in a distorted picture and can never bring a genuine sense of inner meaning.

Meaning is the thought energy that supports all our experiences and it exists in our unconscious and conscious mind. So we have to look inside to find it. The more you search for meaning the more you discover all the structures that make up your mind, emotions and aspirations. Meaning is the currency of consciousness. Everything has meaning, if you can find it. We are all translators and interpreters of meaning.

Each person's meaning is unique. It's crucial that each of us discovers our own special meaning, because this thought energy will bring us the experiences that we need. The search for meaning encourages us to learn how to think skilfully. Skilful thinking creates skilful living, as we discover how to apply the value of meaning in daily life.

Meaningful key moments are those in which we truly know the meaning of our lives, the wonderful moment of enlightenment when we understand what lies behind our actions. Such moments may arrive, not with a fanfare of trumpets, but with the chirp of a bird or a moment of silence.

THE MEANING THOUGHT EXERCISE

Use this exercise if you feel aimless or can't work out what to do in life, or in a specific area of your life, or if you feel stuck and can't move forward in a job or a relationship. Use it also if you want to understand the meaning of something that has happened or if you can't make head or tail of a situation. It can be used also if you are searching for spiritual meaning in your life or having a crisis of faith. It can be used too if you are in the habit of over-analysing and looking for meaning in everything that happens: it will help you to see that we sometimes put meaning on to things that simply don't have any.

Spend twenty minutes once a day doing this exercise.

Sit down in a quiet place in a comfortable chair or in a meditation posture. Close your eyes. Listen. Listen with your ears to the sounds of your body, the sounds of your mind and the sounds in the world around you. Regardless of the sounds and how they make you feel, give thanks for them. Regard them as friends. Listen without any preconceptions, until the sounds merge. Then listen for the thought energy of meaning. It comes as a high-pitched note, or as the sound of a swift-flowing stream. Immerse yourself in this sound. Give thanks for it. Open your eyes and feel the thought energy of meaning in the space around you. Allow it to filter into you. Absorb it. Feel it. Your awareness of the meaning of things has come to life.

James was rapidly becoming famous and successful as a singer. But the faster his success arrived the more he felt isolated and unhappy. James felt that he didn't know who he was or whether he even wanted what he had achieved. He felt he had no meaning in his life. So he began to look for it.

After doing the meaning exercise for three weeks James started to experience connections with his emotions, memories and creativity. He began to see why he had chosen his career and to understand that it was not wealth or success that mattered to him, but the fulfilment of his creativity, giving pleasure to others and his ability to support his family. He began to feel much happier and was able to establish a series of priorities which enabled him to have a successful career and personal life. Instead of feeling at the beck and call of others, he laid down clear guidelines for himself about how he would work and which work he would turn down because it wasn't right for him or interfered with his family life.

Now married and a father, James still uses the meaning exercise every morning as a way to communicate with his inner self. James found his meaning and now can spot the moments when life brings him opportunities to discover deeper lessons.

HAPPINESS

Happiness exists of itself. In the same way that the sun releases warmth for our planet, happiness creates warmth for our lives. Everything is happy. The thought energy of happiness is already formed, we just need to accept it. If you look into a person, you will see it blazing quietly, regardless of their problems. It permeates the air we breathe, it is in nature and all its creatures. You can discover how to be happy when you learn how to think skilfully, because skilful thinking creates skilful living and this releases happiness. And when happiness is released evil and sadness die.

Happiness is its own reward and the joy we feel in moments of pure happiness is unique. Happiness is different for each of us because we all receive thought energy in different ways and we each have our own capacity for receiving and creating happiness.

Happiness is not to be found in the accumulation of material goods or in particular events. True happiness comes from the sacred place within us and as we spend time in this place and increase our capacity for skilful thought energy, so we increase our capacity for happiness.

THE HAPPINESS THOUGHT EXERCISE

This exercise is very simple, safe and yet profound. Many great Tibetan Bön masters used this as their main meditation. Use it if you are unhappy or feel you don't have the capacity for happiness. This exercise is closely connected to the meaning exercise and it is often helpful to do both together. People sometimes feel they need to find meaning in order to be happy, but this is not necessarily true.

Do this exercise for at least ten minutes, first thing in the morning or at any quiet moment through the day.

Sit comfortably and close your eyes. Imagine a fast-flowing stream of light flowing into your heart, pure, brilliant, clear and comfortable. As it touches your heart, you experience the first budding of happiness, which grows stronger and stronger within you. You understand that in everything you do, feel and say in your daily life, happiness will be in you, inspiring and influencing your thoughts and deeds.

Jake didn't believe in happiness. He thought it was for freaks, hippies and the trivial-minded. Jake had no time for happiness, he was a serious man who ran a hardware store and was a pillar in his local community. Then Jake lost his seven-year-old son to meningitis. At this point the seriousness in his life became too much and, filled with grief, he realised the weight of his emotional burdens.

Jake started the exercise and almost instantly he felt huge waves of joy and happiness flow into him. He was able to come to terms with his grief and to rebuild his life. He found answers to personal questions that he hadn't shared with anyone, about the nature of his religious beliefs and the value of his work. Jake added an ice cream parlour on to his hardware store and for two hours a week has free ice cream time for the local children. This has brought his local community together. His happiness has become infectious.

ACCEPTANCE

Acceptance helps us to become empowered and self-aware, to communicate clearly, and to understand kindness. It is the thought energy that leads to compassion, because as acceptance grows so does compassion.

Acceptance is not submissive, it is wise and dynamic because it gives you the courage to know when to accept things, events and people and to know when you have no power to alter them.

We all experience such situations, they are a part of life. Too often we fight against them, refusing to accept what we cannot change. The key moment of acceptance allows us to see when accepting a situation is the wise choice to make. Acceptance removes doubt and gives us insight into the history of our lives. It gives us the power to heal old wounds and to forgive those who have harmed us. It elevates our inner nature and teaches us that all things are possible.

Acceptance is the thought energy of the ever renewing feminine forces of nature and the universe, but it is also the key to discipline, focus and achievement. It does not have a glamorous nature, it is quiet, patient and always present and it is the gateway to living in the energy of the moment, the eternal now.

Acceptance is the hardest of all human qualities to put into action, because acceptance requires us to trust the natural order of life. It means we must give over our daily thoughts to our higher thoughts, to the thought energies that give us the quality and uniqueness of our lives, and for this reason it waits until each of us is ready to acknowledge its presence within us.

THE ACCEPTANCE THOUGHT EXERCISE

Use this exercise if you are finding it hard to accept a situation or event, or if you feel that you are in some way not accepted or acceptable. This may involve a specific person, for instance a mother-in-law who does not accept you, or maybe a general feeling that you are not accepted and are an outsider.

Do this in the evening for at least twenty minutes, as regularly as you can throughout your week.

Sitting in a relaxed position, close your eyes. Now consider the most difficult person or situation that you are dealing with. Let the person or the situation dissolve into a simple white light which you then receive into your heart, where there is no judgement. Feel the lesson this person or situation can teach you. Then do this for the world at large and for your work, relationships, family and any other situations in your life where you need the wisdom of acceptance. Once you have done this, give thanks for the good and bad in your life.

Brian had trouble in dealing with the loss of a long-term relationship with a woman he loved very much. They had been together for six years and he could not let go of her, no matter how hard he tried. This attitude and the pain it caused him started to impact upon his work and friendships with other people. He began to lose friends and his enthusiasm for life. Eventually he lost his job.

When he came to me Brian was feeling very low. As he learned the acceptance exercise, he began to realise how he was destroying his vitality and diminishing his quality of life through his refusal to accept the situation.

Within a few months he had let go of the pain he felt over the separation, and then he let go of his view of the woman he had once loved and began to see her in a new way. He accepted the situation. He accepted her for who she had become. He accepted himself. He became friends with her, he got his old job back and he salvaged his friendships. His fear of living and losing had gone. Acceptance had guided him to a state of inner balance.

INDEPENDENCE

Independence is not the ability to provide for oneself, nor is it being able to manage without other people. Instead independence comes from knowing what your inner problems or issues are, why you have them and how to change them. With independence you are fully able to use your own power and make your life what you wish it to be.

Independence is also the wisdom that comes from understanding the sanctity of life and the divinity that is inside every person, animal and object. The experience of true independence is a key moment in life because it indicates that you have moved into a higher and more secure state of thought and consciousness. Independence also teaches us how the nature of thought works and reveals to us the spiritual laws of nature and of the universe. It teaches us all, as individuals, how to live with each other and to know our responsibilities as members of any community.

Independence enables the soul to grow and your life to become rewarding. It brings us each the skills of living in the world. It teaches us to be responsible for our own actions but also gives us the courage to help others become responsible for their actions.

True independence comes from knowing that we all need each other, but that at the same time we have the power to create our own fate. It teaches us how to act and think with integrity and to live in accordance with our truest beliefs, finding our own inner codes of ethics and behaviour.

This, then, is the essence of independence, the thought

energy of self-knowledge and the responsibilities and joys that come with it.

THE INDEPENDENCE THOUGHT EXERCISE

This meditation puts you in touch with the power of the independence thought energy that exists within you. It is a tangible power that liberates you from feeling lazy, scared or powerless, and puts you in control of your life. Use it if you haven't found your direction in life, if you feel overwhelmed by the world or if you need to take a step forward in life, for instance by leaving home and creating your own adult identity.

Do the exercise in the morning for ten to fifteen minutes, for at least twenty-one days. Results may happen before this time, but doing it for this length of time creates a more balanced outcome.

Sit quietly. Close your eyes. Focus on your navel. As you do this, feel the thought energy of independence, which is everywhere, flow into your body through your navel, filling you with a warm, strong feeling of power and good judgement. As this energy flows, direct it into your physical heart, then into your chest, then up through your body to your forehead, then to the centre of the top of your head, then down the back of your head through your spine, vertebra by vertebra, until it reaches your groin, where it flows into your arms and legs, filling hands, feet, toes and fingers. Your body becomes alive with the thought energy of independence.

Do this circulation of thought energy five times. After this start to see this energy flowing out into your emotional and physical world creating opportunities for independence and success.

Franklin felt that he was always under the control of other people. He was a nice man who found it hard to say no, and people took advantage of this. He felt that he was treated like a doormat and was at the beck and call of others.

This had gone on all his life; his parents had been very dominating and he had always turned to them for advice on how to lead his life. As a result he had no confidence in his own opinions and decisions.

Franklin told me that he wanted to change this, and to be strong and independent. After a week of practising the independence exercise each morning he had a startling experience. The doorman at work, who had always ignored him, suddenly smiled and greeted him politely.

Within two more weeks Franklin found that people were no longer treating him like a doormat. He had changed his energy, he was becoming independent and the world sensed this and started showing him respect. People saw him in a new light and became interested in who he was and not just what he could do for them.

Franklin's talents flourished and were recognised and he gained a senior promotion in the company where he worked. Franklin had begun to see himself as strong and independent, and so others saw him this way too.

DEATH

Death happens to us all and it can come at any time. What do we do when it does come? Panic? Plunge into a state of confusion? Be still and calm? Or do we just try to ignore it and hope it will go away?

People die as they live. So the way you treat your life will indicate the way you will treat your death.

We often do not want to think about death, we find it

scary. Yet death is natural and normal and we have little deaths going on in our lives all the time. The end of the day, the end of a relationship, the end of your favourite TV programme, the end of a job – there are many endings happening all around us every day.

When you die the only thing that will end is the thought energy that kept you alive from the time of your conception. Death is not the absence of life but an interlude in which life rejuvenates itself to move on through a higher state of thought energy. As you die, the thought energy will fade away, until your body empties of it. Your mind, like the loose pages of a book, will be blown gently away, and the very essence of that thought energy which made you who you are, will move on to make a new thought, an addition to what had come before.

Death presents an opportunity to think in a new way. With each death key moment you experience you will find openings too, ways to revitalise and redirect your thinking. Knowing the moments of death in your life brings you the chance for rebirth and rejuvenation.

THE DEATH THOUGHT EXERCISE

When we witness a death, or hear of a death this is a time for us to look at how we understand death in relation to our current circumstances. Use this exercise if you are dying or if you fear death. You can also use it for the death of a project or a relationship or, conversely, if there is something you think should die or end, which is hanging on. You can use it to bless and come to terms with the death of pets or people, but never use it to hasten the death of someone who is lingering in terminal illness. Doing this may cause them to move over into death when they are not yet ready.

Do this exercise for ten minutes a day before bed, for nine days at a time, with three days off before starting again.

Sitting quietly or lying on your back, close your eyes. Think of your body starting to melt into a pool of clear, shining, silver liquid. Take your time. In this pool of liquid, all that is left is your mind, your ability to think and to sense the nature of the thought energy of death. As you start to feel connected to this energy, direct it to remake you again. From the pool of liquid your body is being formed again, this time renewed and vital, with your mind, emotions and thoughts all integrated in a more balanced state than before.

You are connected to the miracle and sacred splendour of the power of the thought energy of death.

Malcolm was rich and achieved a great deal in business. He saw himself as very successful and was always the top dog, until the day when, aged sixty-six, he became sick and learned that he had a very serious brain tumour.

Suddenly he fell to bits. He came to see me when he knew that he didn't have long left to live and he told me that he was terrified of dying. He offered me all his considerable wealth if I could cure him.

I told him that this was not possible or advisable, but that he could choose to come to terms with his death and to have a successful death, giving blessings to those around him. Like so many people Malcolm felt that he had no control over his death or the way he died and he feared a miserable end. When I explained to him that we can always choose to make changes, up until our last breath, he broke down and cried.

After this Malcolm did the death exercise each day, some-

times for long periods of time. It brought him to a successful conclusion in which he overcame his fear of death. He died two months later with a clear mind and a happy heart. He had no grief at dying. His wife told me later that in the moment when she realised he had got to know who he truly was she saw that he was, at last, more genuinely successful than he had ever been and she loved him more deeply than ever before.

BECOMING AWARE OF YOUR KEY MOMENTS

Each of these nine key moments in life is going on around us and within us all the time. Often we only take notice when they build up into a big explosion and go bang in our lives. Yet each of these key moments is a potential force for changing your life. When you recognise the key moment, the change will come. By connecting to the thought energies of each of these nine key moments, and by noticing them in your life day by day, you will find nine pathways that help you on the way to a richer and more fulfilling life. Connecting with them reveals your own strength and ability and helps you to create the life you want.

As you awaken to these nine essential thought energies flowing through everything that you and other people do, you will discover the essence of your life and what you are here on earth to do.

3

YOUR DAILY WORK

In the West it is considered admirable to work long hours and to achieve status, money and power. Ambition is admired and the notion that work takes priority over family, self or leisure is widely accepted.

Men, in particular, are expected to devote all their time and energy to work if they want to succeed – that is, to climb the career ladder and be well paid and respected. Women also come under pressure to have high-powered, paid careers and the idea that a woman might simply want to be a wife and mother, working in the home instead of the workplace, is often treated with scorn. Of course not everyone believes this, and there is a growing movement to change this perception of work, but it is still the dominant view of the Western world that work is the most important aspect of life.

This attitude towards work leads to many problems. Exhaustion, high stress levels and ill health are common. Absenteeism is rife, as workers suffer problems ranging from bad backs to emotional breakdowns. Many people feel torn between their families and their work. Many men grimly accept that they will see little of their children as they grow up, while many women struggle to manage work alongside raising a family.

Few people in the West expect to do work that is satisfying in itself and that they enjoy. Work is a means to an end and that end is money and sometimes power or status. Work is seldom an activity that engenders a sense of pride, well-being and self-esteem.

The Bön view of work is very different. According to ancient Tibetan wisdom, work should be an extension of the family or the community, with each person working to support the community using whatever skills they can contribute. The idea of working for material rewards alone is absent; instead the Bön view is that the nature of work is to interact with others and to benefit from this interaction through heightened vitality.

Work and life away from work should be in perfect balance, each stimulating and acting as a catalyst for the other, like two plants which are cross-fertilising one another. A person may at certain times work long hours, if the job they are doing requires this, but no one should work relentlessly long hours for prolonged periods of time.

The concept of working at a job that is unsatisfying, simply to achieve money, status and power, is alien to the Tibetan view. Of course there are and were people in Bön communities with status and power, but these were conferred for their wisdom and learning and for the contribution they made to the community, and not for working long hours or achieving dominance in the workplace.

The Bön view is that work is a medium in which we can grow, both spiritually and emotionally, and this is the primary benefit to the individual. Through work we experience who we really are. There are aspects of ourselves that we don't even know about, which will appear during the course of our working lives and which, if we see and understand them, will enlighten us. Through our work, things that we need to learn about ourselves and our lives will surface, providing wonderful opportunities for spiritual and emotional growth.

In the meeting of the West and the East the Bön view has

a great deal that is of value to contribute to ideas and beliefs about work. At a time when so many in the West are becoming disillusioned with their working lives and the expectations put upon them, there is a real benefit to be found in taking the ancient wisdom of Bön and applying it to modern working practices.

In this chapter I outline ways to resolve, through skilful thinking, the problems and difficulties you may have with work. Are you doing the right job for you? Working excessive hours? Suffering from stress or ill health? Dealing with workplace bullying, or even being a bully yourself? Are you unappreciated or finding it hard to get on with colleagues? Have you gained financial rewards and status but found yourself spiritually empty?

All these issues can be resolved, simply and effectively. And the power to resolve them lies within you. The skilful use of thought is the most powerful tool you will ever have for positive change. No one need feel trapped, helpless or victimised. Using simple exercises based on ancient rituals, any workplace problem can be solved. And in the process of solving whatever problems you face, you will learn more about yourself and deepen your spirituality.

If you feel scepticism or doubt about your own power to bring about change, using thought alone, that's fine. You don't need to believe in the power of thought, all you need is to be willing to do the appropriate thought exercises and watch the results.

ARE YOU DOING THE RIGHT WORK FOR YOU?

To do work that is wrong for you is the path to misery and frustration. There are examples all around us, of people who hate what they do, or who at best put up with it while feeling their work is too easy, too hard, wrong for them in some way or even dishonest.

There are many reasons why we choose our work. Sometimes the choice is influenced by fear and doubt about our place in the world. Those who doubt their own abilities or who feel uncertain about their place in the world may choose work that appears safe and predictable, even if it is not satisfying. Or they may choose work in which their negative beliefs about themselves are acted out; that is, in which they are treated badly, poorly paid or undervalued.

Work is a means to self-knowledge. Look at the work you do and you will learn how you feel about yourself and where you are in your life at present. This is the most useful guide we can have. If you are unhappy in your work, even if it is well paid or gives you a great deal of power, then earning even more and working even harder will not make you feel better.

It takes courage to recognise that your work is not right for you and to make changes. And when you have to overcome great obstacles in order to make such a change there is an opportunity to extract wisdom from each step along the way. Others may object or encourage you to stay where you are. But it is your own inner voice you must listen to, and your own path that you must follow. Think about what brought you to the work you currently do. Then look at the contribution your work makes to your life as a whole. List the positive and negative effects your work has on your life.

Which is the greater list? Is your deepest impulse to stay, or to go?

How to Find the Right Job

The right job for you will have the following qualities:

1. You will enjoy the work for its own sake as well as for the rewards it brings.

2. Your job will fit into a balanced lifestyle in which your home and family life, self-care and spiritual needs are equally important.

3. Your job will not involve harming anyone or dishonesty of any kind.

4. Your job will use your talents and abilities.

5. Your job will involve working with others in a supportive and harmonious way.

6. Your job will create a sense of contentment in your life and will not involve forced effort or an attempt to fit in.

7. Your beliefs and those of your employer will be in harmony. I don't mean the company mission statement, but the underlying beliefs that underpin the company.

8. Your working environment will be harmonious and pleasant.

Use the Work Thought Exercise below to support you in your search for the right job. In my experience most people know what they'd really like to do, but it simply gets buried under a lot of 'shoulds' and 'oughts'. Look inside yourself and allow it to surface.

Working for Yourself

Being your own boss is something many dream of but few do. It can be exciting, satisfying and rewarding, but the thought energy that motivates you to work for yourself has to be sufficiently powerful to direct you through the hard times as well as the good.

Ask yourself why you want to work for yourself. If money is the only goal then it will not work. Those who are successfully self-employed are motivated by a desire to be responsible, to be original, to create something successful and satisfying and to make their own choices about work and career.

If you feel this way then take the risk, step out into the void and have faith in the energy of your own thoughts. Working in this way is not for everyone. But if it is for you then you will be able to shake off old patterns and to attract new and positive opportunities for changing your life through the blessing of work. Before taking this step do the Work Thought Exercise to discover whether this is the right move for you.

When he came to see me, David had worked in a steel foundry for twenty years. Encouraged by his parents, who felt that job security was all-important, he had started work there when a family friend who ran the foundry offered him a job, soon after he left school.

Although he didn't particularly like the work, David had stayed on and done well. He was promoted, earned a good salary and provided for his wife and children. But deep down David felt that something was wrong. He knew there were aspects of him that were not fulfilled by his job. He wanted to do something else, but had no idea what it could be.

David realised that he was surviving – but not living. There was no joy or passion for him in his job. He was fulfilling his parents' expectations and those of society, but his soul felt empty.

He began doing the Work Thought Exercise and after a few weeks he realised that he needed to leave his job. David had always been creative and had longed to fulfil this side of himself, but felt it was impossible and that he couldn't earn money doing what he really loved. Now he realised it was time to change this unskilful way of thinking, which had brought him such limited rewards, and to direct his skilful thought energy towards creating the career he truly wanted.

With careful financial planning and the support of his wife, he went to art college and today he is a successful, and very happy, potter and ceramic artist.

THE WORK THOUGHT EXERCISE

This exercise can be used in relation to any work problem, issue, puzzle or conflict. It is extremely effective and powerful and, when used consistently, produces rapid results. Therefore if you only do one exercise in relation to your work, make it this one. You can use it often; many of my clients use it on a regular basis to solve any work difficulties or questions that arise. The exercise will enable you to gather information and insight, to stop unskilful and negative actions and events, to create positive change and to develop success. When using this exercise it is important to be responsible in the way you apply it and to be aware of the nature of the problem you are dealing with.

Sit comfortably on the floor or on a chair. Close your eyes. Listen to your breathing for a few minutes.

Now focus your thoughts completely upon your work problem or query. In your mind's eye you begin to see this problem or query start to take on the shape of a small silver reflecting globe. Fill this globe with all your focus and attention. As it fills see it change from a reflective silver globe into a dark blue pulsing globe.

Now, in your mind, fire the globe at an amazing speed towards the problem or query you have focused upon. See it penetrate every layer of the problem. At the same time as you send the globe off at the speed of thought, open your eyes and blow your breath out through your mouth, gently and deliberately.

Once this globe has done its work it will return to you with answers, solutions and empowerment. It may take a few days before it pops back into your mind. It could take a few minutes. It depends upon the subject matter.

When it returns, see the globe open up into four segments within all the thought energies it has collected. Breathe them into you by breathing in and as you breathe out think of them becoming part of you and they will then become information, which you can understand and use.

OVERWORK

Overworking is a massive problem in the Western world. During the last thirty years the culture of 'workaholism' has become endemic and many employers have come to expect employees to work excessive hours as a matter of course. People who work too long and too hard usually over-identify with their work. In other words they think that their work is who they are. If their work disappeared they would be unsure of their identity and would find themselves in crisis, with no true sense of self or their direction in life.

The more you identify with your work the more you lose access to your inner thought energies and the further you drift from the possibility of discovering your inner spiritual potential. Those who overwork are trying to control the nature of things. Work has only the value you give it and needs to be kept in its true perspective. Those who overwork and over-identify with work lead unbalanced lives in which their personal lives and those close to them, their families and friends, suffer.

If your career takes up most of your time, your life and your vitality then you will burn yourself out. To be creative and vital in your job it is important to understand which parts of your personality can contribute to work and which parts need to be cultivated for personal living only. When you begin to release your identification with work you will be able to reclaim large amounts of thought energy which you can redirect back to your inner world in order to improve the quality of your life.

Overworkers are often reacting to their work environment, which has an energy that draws them in and holds them there.

How to Stop Overworking

Begin to notice how you feel when you arrive at work and when you leave. What kind of energy is around, what effect does your workplace have on you? It is likely that you are reacting in a conditioned way to your work environment, which has a powerful energy pulling you towards it. If this is the case then you can send out thought energy which will purify your workplace.

Sit quietly and for several minutes visualise a fire, burning all the negative energy out of your office and leaving it pristine and cleansed, ready for new, skilful thought energies to fill it. Repeat this daily until you no longer feel the energy of your workplace pulling you. Once you are freed from this you will be able to change your lifestyle and refuse to overwork.

Thea was a highly successful lawyer who, at a very young age, became a partner in the firm she worked for. This meant a great deal to Thea, who began to work even longer hours than she had before. The more she worked the more work she took on and the more there was to do. Some of the assistants at work joked about whether Thea ever actually went home at night, as she was always there.

Thea was engaged to a man she'd met at college. He was a doctor, but unlike Thea he did not allow work to take over his life. He became increasingly frustrated with her obsession with work. On the rare evenings when she wasn't working she talked about work and brought work home with her. Even at parties and social gatherings Thea talked almost exclusively about her work. Finally Thea's fiancé broke off their engagement, telling her that he could not marry someone whose work was their life. He wanted time for their relationship, for children and for fun together.

Thea was shocked and distraught. She loved her fiancé and didn't want to lose him. But she loved her job too, and couldn't imagine life without it.

I asked Thea to pay attention to the energy around her work, and she soon began to feel the powerful pull her office was exerting towards her. Thea sent out purifying energy towards her office for several days and began to feel differently whenever she arrived there.

In addition she also did the Work Thought Exercise. She became very honest with herself about her attitude and beliefs and eventually was able to release her over-identification with her work. Gradually she began to understand that she could still be valued at work and contribute her share by working more reasonable hours. The more she did this the more she found her vital energy, which had been very low, return to her. She began to develop her interests outside work, to stop talking and thinking exclusively about work and to see that work was simply a part of her life, not the whole of it.

After six months her fiancé, delighted by the change in her, returned to her and they were able to look forward to a far happier and more balanced life together.

THE USE AND ABUSE OF POWER

In the course of my practice I see many highly successful and powerful people. Some of them run companies or corporations, some have achieved fame and others enjoy wielding great influence in government. Most of them have made a great deal of money and enjoy all the status symbols that wealth can bring: large homes, fast cars and international travel.

What is interesting is that some of these people are happy in their work and others are not. Some of those I see may come to me for a health or emotional problem, but are essentially comfortable with what they are doing. Others are deeply unhappy. Their wealth and status has come to feel like a burden, they are ill, their private lives are often disastrous and they feel unfulfilled and empty.

What is it that makes the difference between these two groups? Certainly not the nature of their jobs or the degree of their wealth or success. What makes the difference is the way they do their jobs. Let me illustrate this point with two examples.

John was at the very top of a large business corporation. He had worked his way to the top very fast and had earned himself a great deal of money. John believed that the company's success was due to his efforts. He saw himself as beyond reproach and as superior to others. John had put himself on a pedestal and expected others to pay homage to him. He seldom praised or valued his staff, instead he interfered with everyone's work and made it clear that he couldn't trust anyone, even senior managers, to do their job well. He even blamed others for his own errors. His manner was arrogant and haughty, he didn't hesitate to yell at staff in front of others or to belittle them and he expected them to work long hours and to put the company before their families.

Needless to say John was not liked. Those who worked closely with him pretended to like him, but he knew that he had no real friends at work and he felt very isolated. John had always felt that this didn't matter, as long as people feared him and did what he wanted and the company prospered.

Things changed the day his personal assistant told John that she was leaving because she could no longer stand his bullying, brutish methods. For the first time someone had stood up to him and it shocked John.

When he came to see me, looking tense and angry, he told me he knew he was hated and thought it didn't matter, but he'd come to realise that it did. He got no genuine pleasure from being alone at the top and from making other people's lives miserable. As we talked John recognised that he'd actually been unhappy for years and didn't enjoy his job. He'd been forcing himself to keep going, and taking his unhappiness out on everyone around him.

A month later John resigned and took a year off to travel, spend time with his wife and reflect. During this time he decided to take up charity work, something he could afford to do as he had no need to work again. When I last saw him John was working for a children's charity and was a relaxed and contented man.

Max was the chief executive officer of a very successful motor company which produced luxurious top-of-the-range cars. It had been his boyhood dream to work for this company ever since, when he was eight years old, a friend of his father's had owned one of their cars and allowed him to sit in it. Max couldn't believe that he had a job that allowed him to drive these fabulous cars and this enthusiasm never faded.

Max believed that work should be fun for everyone and that his staff should have as much support as possible. He installed a company crèche and gave everyone flexible working hours. He banished suits and ties for a more informal style and made sure that everyone, no matter what their job, had a go at tinkering with the cars. Once a year he and his directors spent a day on the production line, while the staff spent a day coming up with management ideas.

Max never let anyone work long hours and was available to listen if any of his employees had a problem. Everyone who worked for him loved the job and people stayed with the company for a long time. In some cases whole families worked for him.

Max came to see me because he was exhausted; he had been looking after everyone else and neglecting himself. He needed to follow his own rules and cut back his hours, which he did. This minor adjustment was all that was required, because Max was extremely happy in his job and had no wish to leave. His money and success were not the cause of his happiness; his delight in the job and pleasure in running a good and caring company were what really mattered to him.

It's easy to see why John was unhappy and Max was happy at work. John's problem was his overbearing and demanding style. He was abusing the power that he had. Power, like money, is a currency that is used to exchange ideas, actions, thoughts and outcomes. Used in the wrong way power will never bring security or rewards.

In the workplace power is only useful if it helps you to create effective change which goes beyond your own interests and is of obvious benefit to everyone. This was the way in which Max successfully used his power.

STRESS

It is impossible to avoid all stress; it is simply a part of the human condition that there are, from time to time, stresses that cause us to feel under pressure. Stress is not, in itself, a bad thing. It can be energising, motivating and exciting. Reaching a goal or deadline, achieving a deal, coping with a new job and organising others can all be stressful in positive ways.

Stress becomes negative when it begins to feel overwhelming and cause unhappiness. This is when it's important to recognise and contain it. Negative stress may come from the behaviour of others, from unreasonable demands, from pressure you put on yourself to achieve or from unhappiness with your work.

According to Bön wisdom stress is simply another form of unskilful thought energy and it is your reaction to it that determines its effect on you. If you are identifying with other people's negative thought energy, in other words their fears, worries and expectations, then this may cause you a great deal of stress. Stress can become addictive if it is repeated often enough. If you are feeling stress regularly it's important to recognise it and make changes. You can choose to deal with stress and to work in a peaceful and harmonious way, which will in turn lead to greater productivity, creativity and success.

What's important is to recognise situations and people that are affecting you negatively and to take steps to deal with them. Negative stress creates emotional, physical, intellectual and spiritual problems. It is vital that you help yourself, rather than waiting for the situation to change or for your employer, or anyone else, to change things. You have within you the skill and ability to change your thoughts and your life in whatever ways you need.

Use the Stress Ransom Ritual and the Work Thought Exercise to change the inner nature of your thought energy and banish stress.

THE STRESS RANSOM RITUAL

Sit quietly and then picture the stress and unhappiness you feel. It might be an individual, a situation or your job as a whole. Concentrate on this and then face it head on in a confrontation and challenge it. Now ransom the unskilful thought of stress, literally steal it away in your mind and give it an ultimatum. Let it know that it must release the inner wisdom it is strangling, instantly and never trouble you again. Tell it that it can have its life back only if it then disappears and releases its hold on your wisdom.

This is what I call the zero-tolerance approach to stress and its results are instant. After doing this exercise you will experience a physical or emotional sign that the exercise has worked. Your inner wisdom, freed from its prison, will be able to help and support you in making the decisions and changes you need.

Adrian worked for a very famous software company where he managed many new projects and was responsible for a lot of staff. Everyone in his company had huge admiration for him. He took his work very seriously and felt a strong sense of responsibility to both the company and the employees under his care. He was always the first person to arrive in the office and the last person to leave. He would even work at weekends and his family hardly ever saw him.

But after fifteen years of this Adrian was not in a good state. His concentration was poor, he had lost his sense of humour, he had put on weight, had mood swings, crying fits and periods of lethargy. He managed to keep these symptoms hidden at work, but could not hide them at home, and his wife became more and more worried.

Eventually, in desperation, his wife brought him to see me. Although he had been reluctant to come, he soon began to talk. He told me that he felt he owed his company everything. He had started there with no formal education and had enjoyed success as it grew. Now he felt exhausted and burned out. He could no longer do his job properly and he felt he was letting everyone down. He didn't want to give up work or switch to another job; he liked the company and the financial security of his job was very important to him.

Adrian was suffering from severe stress. His life was out of balance and he needed to make changes, and as we talked he began to see that he had many choices and options.

I encouraged him to do the Stress Ransom Ritual and the Work Thought Exercise and although he was uncertain about whether they would be of value, he agreed.

A week later Adrian told me that, although he had found it difficult to sit quietly and concentrate, even for a few minutes, he had persevered with the exercises every day and had begun to feel the results. He felt calmer, more optimistic and more in control than he had for a long time.

As he continued to do the exercises over the following weeks Adrian began to make changes to his working life. He cut back his hours and stopped working at weekends. He no longer stayed until everyone else had left and he learned to delegate many tasks which he had taken on himself unnecessarily and to give his colleagues more responsibility. He began to enjoy spending more time with his wife and children and to look forward to having fun with them at the weekends.

Six months on Adrian was a changed man. His stress symptoms had disappeared and he appeared relaxed and at ease with himself.

BULLYING

Although it is seldom spoken about, a great deal of bullying takes place in the workplace. Colleagues can bully one another, and sadly many bosses, who should set an example of kind and compassionate behaviour, are also bullies. When bullying is occurring then the two sides, the bully and the person being bullied, are experiencing two different parts of the same unskilful thought energy. This energy is fear or anger.

Bullying is bad for everyone in the workplace, whether they are directly involved in it or not. Every part of the working community is affected. Bullies cause misery as they aim to discredit or harm their victim.

Often people reveal themselves in the workplace more truthfully than they do in other aspects of their lives. Work is the place where we act out all that we need to learn and all that we know and essentially are.

The bullied and the bully attract each other to play out a role, both actors in a script that they don't really understand, both channelling the fear or anger that exists in the workplace and their own fearful, angry thoughts. They lock themselves into a battle of survival and as this continues they both lose a little of themselves each day, as do those who work with them and the organisation they work for. This process is played out everywhere from small shops to multinational companies.

Are You a Bully?

It is never easy to admit that you are a bully. It requires courage to take such a step. But it is vital, because the act of bullying causes so much damage. If you are behaving in a bullying way then you will probably know it. If you are not certain then look for the following indicators:

1. Frequent changes in mood.

2. Losing your temper often with colleagues and then apologising afterwards.

3. Refusing to listen to others' viewpoints.

4. Behaving in a demanding or over-forceful way.

If you think that you might be a bully then you need to understand that you have separated yourself from the sacredness of life and you are passing your fear and anger on to others by your thoughts and actions.

You can heal the heartache which is at the root of your behaviour and rediscover your compassion for others by using the following ritual.

THE PURIFICATION RITUAL

This is a simplified version of a ritual used by ancient Tibetans to purify someone who had behaved in a cruel or bullying way to others. This was taken extremely seriously by the Tibetans, who considered severe bullying to be as serious as rape. They would also use this ritual on both parties in any kind of dispute or fight.

Take a bowl and place in it a piece of self-lighting charcoal. Sprinkle it with juniper essential oil (the Tibetans used juniper branches on a fire). Juniper has remarkable cleansing and purifying powers: it clears thought pollutions and obstructions and cleanses the mind, body and environment. You can use a juniper twig, if you have one, but light it carefully as it flares up very fast. Light the charcoal and then, as it begins to smoke, waft the smoke and juniper fumes all around your body. It will cleanse you of any desire to hurt others, to bully or to create pain. You will be left with a sense of peace and a desire to express only kindness to others.

Lydia was a high-powered boss in an advertising agency who came to see me because of health problems. As we talked and I asked about her work it became clear that Lydia was a strong and determined woman who took a very rigid view of the work situation and how everyone should behave.

When I asked Lydia if she thought her behaviour at work could be considered bullying she was surprised and insisted it wasn't. But on her next visit she told me she had thought about what I'd said and realised that, although she didn't intend to hurt others, she was behaving in an aggressive and bullying way towards her subordinates. She had no tolerance for personal problems and gave no leeway to herself or others. As she spoke of this Lydia began to cry. Her rigid attitude had been hurting herself, as well as others, and had led, in part, to her health problems.

Lydia carried out the purification ritual and told me that she felt a great sense of happiness and peace settle over her. When she returned to work, a few days later, she was able to take a softer, more generous attitude and this led to a much happier relationship with those who worked for her.

Are You Being Bullied?

Bosses who bully are not leaders but followers. They are people who follow their unskilful thought energies and are behaving in a way that is essentially selfish. This selfishness involves dumping their unskilful thought energy on others over whom they have power. Such people are often unaware of the misery they cause. They have isolated themselves from their ability to give and receive compassion and spiritual love to others.

When co-workers bully one another it is because they are insecure in their work and in their lives. Often the underlying unskilful thought energy that causes this kind of bullying is anger, and anger, like the common cold, can be catching. Thought energy can spread among co-workers, so that people start to experience one another's thought energy. The bully passes on anger, the anger stings the person being bullied and he or she then bottles it up and passes it on to someone else, at work or outside the workplace, at home or even to a total stranger in a shop or on a bus or train.

Often when a co-worker is bullying another, other workers pick up on this and also begin to dump their thought energies on the unfortunate victim. This may not necessarily be in the form of blatant bullying, they may simply find a way to unload their thoughts or emotions on to the person, which of course they have no right to do.

Dealing with Bullying

First, think about whether there is anything that you have contributed to the situation to collude with or encourage the bullying. This needs to be addressed. Do you need to change your own thought processes and behaviour?

Second, start to create mental clarity around the work you do. See each work action that you carry out throughout your day bringing you empowerment, success and wisdom.

Third, use your thoughts to direct as much compassion as possible towards the bullies. This is an impersonal compassion generated by your thoughts, not by your emotions. It is detached, focused and stern. As you continue to do this it will create a distance between the bully and you and you will gain strength, courage and insight.

Fourth, if you are being dumped on by others, either as direct bullying or simply as offloading thoughts and emotions which then become a burden to you, begin to direct the negative thought energy back along the chain of bullying. As soon as any incident happens imagine yourself gathering up the energy in the situation and sending it back, through each person in the chain, until it reaches the person who started the bullying. The returned thought energy will gather around the bully and stay with them until they begin to experience the suffering they have caused and stop bullying.

This redirection of the unskilful thought energy can work quickly and effectively, but it requires sincerity and intensity in your own skilful thinking. Returning this unskilful thought energy to the bully will prove more effective than emotional explosions, physical violence or repeated complaining, all of which will simply give more energy to the bully.

Honey worked as a secretary in an advertising agency. All was going well until, three months after she arrived, the bullying started. Her boss began by teasing her about her name. At first she didn't mind, but after a while it became annoying. The teasing became sexual and then, when she did not respond, there were caustic comments about her work and intelligence. He teased her about being blonde and called her stupid.

Other co-workers were witnesses to all this, but no one said anything.

Honey started to feel ill, wondered if the things her boss was saying were true. She lost confidence and started to hate going to work. She even dreamed about the bullying.

When Honey came to me she was physically unwell as well as deeply unhappy. After receiving Tibetan medical treatment, including massage, herbs and acupuncture, I taught her the Work Thought Exercise. As soon as she started doing this, she felt energy and courage returning to her. Honey also began to direct compassionate thoughts towards her boss.

Then one night Honey had to work late and her boss made advances to her. With dignity she said nothing and walked away. Shortly afterwards she was fired. Instead of crying or feeling sorry for herself, Honey complained directly to the managing director. At first he refused to see her, but Honey persisted and told him her story. He told her he would consider everything.

A month later Honey was invited to return to work and found that her boss had gone. Three years later she is a boss herself, and a good one. Honey believes she found the courage to fight back and change things as a result of the work Thought Exercise, which made her thoughts clear, precise, compassionate, powerful and effective. She uses this Work Thought Exercise today to help solve disputes and problems at work.

FEELING UNDERVALUED

If you feel unappreciated and undervalued at work then you are probably suffering from the 'poor me' syndrome.

Feeling temporarily undervalued is one thing, and this is usually quickly resolved by talking to the appropriate person or, if necessary, changing jobs. But if this is a long-term situation for you then there is more to it than an unappreciative boss.

Complaining is damaging because words are the houses in which our thoughts live. The way you speak will indicate the way you think.

In the Tibetan view a person who constantly complains to others about their lot, who feels sorry for themselves and who blames others (e.g. the boss, colleagues) is creating and spreading powerful negative thought energy. The more you think in this way the more this thought energy will entrap you and ensure that your situation never improves.

The people around such a person soon begin to treat them badly, just as they expect, or to avoid them altogether. This is because the echo of such negative thought energy bounces back to you and affects you to a greater and greater extent. You are creating a thought cancer which is very destructive. Those who work around such a person often feel sick, unhappy and tired as a result of the impact of this thought energy.

However, it is possible to protect yourself from this energy, if you are affected by it, and to heal it if you are the person trapped in self-pity.

To avoid 'poor me' thought energy

Focus all your attention on the 'poor me' person. With heartfelt intention, gaze beyond what they are saying and the sound of their voice until you see, behind this exterior, a place inside this person which is begging for love.

Now send a thought missile, or thought bomb, known in Tibet as a Zor, which blows to bits the nagging and complaining behaviour of the person. This will be a soft and gentle explosion, which takes place over days and weeks rather than instantly. While you send the Zor you can give it a time limit in which to work.

To alter 'poor me' thought energy

Do this exercise for ten minutes each morning before work.

Focus on the nature of your speech and the sound of your voice and notice the words and phrases you use. Now direct the thought energy of peace and contentment towards your complaints and allow yourself to feel that everything is okay in the world and that things are as they should be.

After doing this you will find that you lose the desire to complain and that you're only interested in talking about good news.

When Thomas first came to see me he was working for an insurance agency as a clerk. He didn't particularly like his work, but felt he would be happy if only his boss would appreciate him properly. Thomas was desperate for approval and spent his time at work looking for signs that his boss liked or disliked him and reading all sorts of false meanings into every situation.

Thomas spent his lunch hours with the other clerks complaining about his thoughtless, unappreciative boss. He told anyone who would listen about how hard he worked and how undervalued he was. Gradually his colleagues began to be fed up with this and to stop making helpful suggestions. Soon Thomas found himself lunching alone and feeling even more sorry for himself. At the same time his boss became irritated by Thomas's ingratiating manner and began to be more abrupt with him and to avoid him.

Thomas had no idea what he was doing wrong. In fact he thought he was doing everything right. It was only when we talked that he began to see the pattern he was creating and he told me that he'd been in a similar situation in his previous job.

Thomas began the exercise to alter 'poor me' thought energy and found that within a month things were beginning to change at work. As his desire to complain disappeared his colleagues began to include him again and his boss became warmer. Thomas's longing for approval dissolved and he was able to appreciate and value himself and to be responsible for his own happiness at work.

WORKMATES – OR ENEMIES?

Relationships with others at work can often be loaded with hidden agendas, caused by the working environment. Work friendships often involve complex issues of trust, emotional security and communication, as well as fear. For this reason they can often be fraught, tense or difficult.

To create appropriate relationships and friendships take your time and first observe people. Then create a direct thought energy about each person that you interact with. To do this you need to follow your gut instinct about each person you meet. If your first thought is This is a good person, or I don't think I can trust this person, then hold that thought energy. Each time you come in contact with that person re-activate and send out the thought energy you have about them. This will automatically let you know the right approach, how you need to treat the person, the best way of connecting with them and where the appropriate boundaries are in your contact with them.

For instance, if you feel that you are unable to trust someone, then reactivating that thought energy will ensure that you don't confide in them inappropriately, or entrust them with important tasks or information.

It may be that you change your mind about someone further into the relationship, when they have shown you other qualities. But your first feeling is the right one to follow until you have more information.

Ten Ways to Improve Your Work and Career through Skilful Thinking

Use these guidelines to create greater happiness and harmony in your work at all times.

1. Each morning before work, sit down and focus your thought energy on one thought that leads to a deed or action, no matter how big or small. Remember that in Tibetan

wisdom a thought is a deed. If you focus on the thought then you will carry out the deed and in this way you will discover that you can achieve anything by beginning with the thought.

2. Always communicate with every person at work, whether senior or junior, with equal regard, simplicity and respect, regardless of how they treat you. Polite communication creates open hearts.

3. Never disregard any thought, small or large, in regard to your work. Every thought is valid and deserves attention. Examine the thought to see whether it holds valuable information and will bear fruit.

4. If you are a member of a team, then bring creativity to your co-workers. While remaining compassionate and modest, never be afraid to say what you think. When you do this others will then seek out your input.

5. Never involve yourself in a work-related problem unless you have direct involvement or you feel it morally right to defend someone. Do this with clarity and thought.

6. Always be punctual for everything. Punctuality means you respect others, but more importantly it means you respect yourself. And if you respect yourself in this way people will come to respect you.

7. Share your knowledge with those who are sincere in their wish to learn. Be aware of those who wish to undermine you or play politics. In sharing knowledge you can create thought marks on your ideas, so that if anyone steals them, no matter how hard they try, they will not be able

to use them without your involvement. A thought mark is like a blueprint; simply visualise your personal stamp on your idea and include the length of time you wish it to apply for.

8. The workplace is a community and as in every community there must be rules. Create rules within yourself on how to deal with rude or difficult people. Trust your own instinct and use as your guideline the way you would wish to be treated by others.

9. Personalise your workspace. If you can, bring something of yourself from home to your work so that you can imbue your workspace or office with your own thought energies and personal power.

10. See all your activities, thoughts, actions and deeds at work and in your career as opportunities for spiritual development. At the end of each day take five minutes to consider if you can leave your work with an easy heart.

WORKING WISDOM

Always show compassion and kindness in the workplace and in your work and career communications. Help other people to help themselves. Kindness and compassion bring meaning to work and spread a sense of equality. When you contribute in this way you will begin to delight in your own humanity. Skilful thinking creates skilful living and this is as important at work as elsewhere in your life.

Working wisdom, based on kindness and compassion, is the basis for any work-related skill and helps you to grow and to gain self-knowledge. Always set yourself high standards and do your work for yourself, not simply to please others. High standards enable your mind to clear.

By applying skilful thinking to the way you communicate with others, you will discover how to communicate with the heart and soul of each person you encounter.

Working wisdom shows you how to discover all your potential and use it for the purpose of benefiting yourself and others. Allow your wisdom at work to shine so that everyone can see your brilliance.

Be wise, think well, work well and you shall be well.

4

THE TRUE VALUE OF MONEY

From birth we grow up accepting that money is part of life. Money has an ancient association with mankind; we have always used some form of barter or trade. Since the earliest forms of trade and civilisation, money has represented the human desire to create, build and control our environment.

In the Tibetan Bön view what matters most is not money itself but the thought energy behind it, because this thought energy has a profound influence over us. It is not money that makes the world go round, but the thought energy of money, which is enormously powerful.

According to Tibetan beliefs the forms of money we use will evolve and change, but the energy behind it will remain the same and will continue to influence us powerfully. Therefore it is vital for us truly to know and understand this thought energy and to use it skilfully for the benefit of others as well as ourselves. With the ability to use the thought energy of money skilfully will come prosperity. Money does not create happiness, but it can lessen suffering and help to create the conditions for happiness. However, in order to improve our material circumstances and be free from want we must use the thought energy of money with skill and care. Money thought energy has its own set of morals and rules that must be followed.

The skilful thought energy of money involves the ability to attract money to you, and then to use it with wisdom and generosity. It involves knowing how much is enough for you and refusing to identify yourself with money, however much or little you have. In the Bön view money should never be acquired selfishly or thoughtlessly – if it is it will soon be lost again, or will bring unhappiness. Money must always be used for the greater good of all, and acquired in ways that involve the good of all.

The use of money has gone from being a power isolated from most people, as it was in ancient days, to an emotionally charged everyday experience for all of us. Money has become accessible to nearly everyone and using it is therefore a common experience, behind which is enormous global thought power. The money in your pocket, or in your bank account, as well as the money that you want or need, holds all of humanity's emotions and thoughts to do with money. Because it represents such powerful energy, money is the great instructor of sacred truths in the material world. It is through money that we learn important truths about ourselves.

In order to have a practical and spiritual understanding of money and to use it wisely, you must first discover your relationship with it and your thoughts, emotions and beliefs about money. When you do this, the thought energy of money will start to work for you rather than against you and you will be able to create true prosperity in your life, spiritual as well as financial. In coming to understand the thought energy of money you will discover the nature of your own connections to the material world. And through doing this you can learn the wisdom of materialism and its place in contributing to your spiritual development.

In this chapter I will explain the addictive aspect of money thought energy and the importance of overcoming the fear of poverty and of money itself, which dominates so many people today, creating unhappiness and want. I will also explain how to use money thought energy skilfully and, through the use of simple exercises, how to create lasting and worthwhile prosperity in your life.

THE VALUE OF MONEY

What is the true value of money? From the ancient Tibetan Bön view, the true value of money is the use of thought energy to achieve a physical result. In other words, its value lies in the way we think about it and the prosperity or lack we create as a result of this skilful or unskilful thinking.

Each of us has a personal and family history connected with money, and this also affects the value we give it. Money may have been unimportant in your family, or it may have been very important indeed. Depending upon this history, we invest in money through our emotions and our actions. To find out what value you give to money reflect on it for a while and see how you feel.

- How would you feel about losing all the money you have?
- Are you desperate for more money than you have?
- How easily do you share or give away the money you have?

The answers to these questions will help you to understand the value you put on money.

Whenever you lose money, make money, receive money as a gift or prize, or earn money by working, the money that you gain or lose comes to you from inner thought energy that has been developing within you since you were first conceived. So, what you have right now is directly related to your inner thought energy about money and will give you a clear indication of how skilful or unskilful this thought energy is.

Your underlying thoughts about your money, how you relate to it, and what you want to do with it are crucial to how you keep it or lose it. It is easy to fall into unskilful thinking patterns around money. Remember, money is not dishonest, greedy, tight-fisted, or undeserving, but the thoughts behind it can be. Each one of us can change unskilful thought energy around money at any time. You can create more money than you have currently, as long as you do it in a calm, positive and balanced way.

OVER-IDENTIFICATION WITH MONEY

As the world becomes a smaller place, our collective anxiety about money and security grows. This comes about because increasing numbers of people believe and trust in money more than they do in themselves. The thought energy of money has an addictive side, which demands total absorption in itself. And this can result in this kind of over-identification with money, so that people come to believe they *are* their money and that the amount of money they have is the measure of who they are and their own personal value.

It is very easy to over-identify with money and to be controlled by this influence. Everyone, at some time, does this – from the poorest person to the richest.

Answer the following questions:

1. Do you feel consistently anxious about money?

2. Is poverty your greatest fear?

3. Are your key ambitions and goals in life connected with money?

4. Do you think constantly about how much money you have and check it daily?

5. Does spending money cheer you up when you feel low?

6. Do you judge things by their cost?

7. Do you stick your head in the sand around money, ignoring bills and bank statements?

8. Do you believe that having lots of money would make you happy?

9. Do you think any job is worth doing if the pay is high enough?

10. Do you believe that you don't really deserve lots of money?

The more yes answers you gave, the greater your identification with money. If you answered yes more than five times then you are over-identifying with money to the point where it is damaging the rest of your life.

When you over-identify with money – which is easy to do in the very strongly material West – then you are likely to have problems with money, including debt, foolish spending or investment, being driven by the desire for money or meanness with money.

To have a healthy and productive relationship with money it is important to understand that money is completely separate from who you are. You are not your credit rating, your bank balance or your debts. To forget this is the origin of mental and spiritual poverty, and this in turn leads to becoming trapped by the demands of survival. Money can and does make people unhappy even when they have a lot of it, if they believe that they are nothing without their money.

Money is an emotional force that needs to be treated with care and respect because the thought energy behind money loves to own those who use it unskilfully.

Never be so bound up with money that you believe you are your money. Know who you are and that your money, whether you have a lot or a little, is quite separate.

Laurence was a rich man, who had enjoyed making his money and who loved to play with it every day, moving sums from one account to another and switching investments, simply for the pleasure of making more money than he could ever spend.

One day Laurence took a risk that was too big, and lost all his money. The shock turned his hair white almost overnight and left him looking old and ill. He was still only forty-seven, but he could hardly bring himself to get out of bed in the morning. His life felt aimless and he was terribly sorry for himself.

Laurence's wife Francine coped with the crisis in quite a different way. Although she had enjoyed being rich, she did not mind being poor. She felt lucky to have her health, her husband and children and a home. She had not worked for some years, but now she went out and got a job and kept the family running. While Laurence bemoaned his bad luck and wept with self-pity, Francine discovered her talent for selling and made new friends in her job.

It was only when Francine got fed up with his behaviour and threatened to leave him that Laurence took a long hard look at himself. He began to see that he had lived for his money and that all his self-worth was tied up with it. Without money he saw himself as a hopeless failure.

He saw how his wife, who had not over-identified with their money, had dealt with things quite differently.

Humbled by her cheerfulness and courage, he picked himself up and began again, opening a small business dealing in antiques, which had once been his hobby.

Together Francine and Laurence rebuilt their lives and changed their priorities. Today they are not rich, but they have everything they need, and they are happy.

FEAR OF POVERTY

The fear of poverty that so many people have is an ancient fear inherited from previous generations. In the West few people suffer from true poverty – that is, a lack of the basic essentials necessary for survival. But many people feel themselves to be poor because we live in a society where the pressure to be rich and to own many possessions is great. Many more live in fear of losing what they have, so that rather than enjoying it they cling to it like a drowning man to a rock. Fear of poverty attracts poverty and can stop us from creating a life of financial security, emotional balance and spiritual happiness.

When you fear poverty you become trapped by obstacles that are attracted to your inner unskilful thought energy, blocking you from prosperity and material and spiritual success. It is important to remove these obstacles from within and to free yourself from the fear of poverty, which can create great stress and unhappiness. The fear of poverty affects not just individuals but mankind as a whole. Businesses, large and small, banks and whole communities are affected by this fear when it is powerful enough.

Poverty and its attendant obstacles take on many forms and because all the people of the human race share the same planet, poverty shifts like the seasons from one form to another. As the poverty-stricken peoples of Africa experience physical deprivation, so poverty in other places takes on an emotional and spiritual form. In the West, though most people have shelter and enough to eat, there is a great deal of spiritual poverty.

Poverty is thought energy of an intense and ancient significance and, as with war, it is a thought energy that connects us all directly. All of us are linked by our own personal thoughts, the thought energies of the ancient and recent past, the present, and the possible future that awaits us. It is vital, therefore, that all of us work to overcome the fear of poverty both in ourselves and in the world. When we turn away from the plight of others, we turn away from ourselves. When we overcome the fear of poverty in ourselves then we contribute to overcoming it in the world. We can help those who suffer physical poverty not just by giving food, medication, education, peace-making and political intervention but through the use of skilful thought energies to support them and create prosperity.

THOUGHT EXERCISE FOR OVERCOMING THE FEAR OF POVERTY

Sit quietly and close your eyes. Focus your mind on the rise and fall of your breath. Allow this rhythm to relax your body and calm your mind. Focus on this calm state for several minutes. Then when you are ready, slowly open your eyes and read the following invocation aloud. Speak each line, including the title, with care and passion.

Say this invocation twice a day when you need to overcome the fear of poverty, and in time try to memorise it. The invocation will also be effective for other kinds of problems or obstacles, as many problems stem from the fear of poverty.

INVOCATION FOR THE REMOVAL OF OBSTACLES

My heart beats, as all hearts do,
But for a short time,
I breathe, as all beings do,
But for a short time,
I cast out my fears, my obstacles,
I cast away all negativity!
I cast away all poverty!
I trample down and crush all obstructions!
I awaken my heart,
The heart of endless blessings
That dwells within me,
Here I call upon my inner power
To make me fearless.

(Clap your hands together with force three times slowly)

May all obstacles be removed from this world.

(Repeat the line above five times)

(Clap your hands together with force three times slowly)

May blessings and compassion be the fruits for all beings.
Let me take the obstacles of others as my own
that they may live in happiness and peace.

(Clap your hands together with force three times slowly)

I call to me now the forces of abundance washed
by compassion and light.
This brings forth all that I need.
I summon and invoke
the power of the thoughts of prosperity within me.
Now, Now, Now, Now!
I send them out to change my world and bring me

My intent and aims.
Each thought creates abundance for me in
mind, body, spirit
Through thought, speech and action.

(Clap hands loudly three times)

This I create
With my full thoughtful aim and purpose
So that I and others may no longer be bound by fear.

(Clap hands loudly three times)

Jennie was a teacher who lived in a constant state of fear of poverty. This fear created many obstacles in her life, both financial and spiritual. Eventually it became so powerful that it drove away friends, personal relationships, the enjoyment of her work and her chance for happiness.

When Jennie came to see me she was in debt, had recently been left by her lover, she had failed to get a job she really wanted and a friend had betrayed her. She was deeply unhappy and didn't understand why these things should happen to her.

When we talked Jennie began to understand how her fear of poverty had started in childhood, when her parents lived in constant debt, and had come to influence her adult life. She feared that she could not have what she wanted, in every area of her life, and so it became true.

Within two days of using this invocation, Jennie's life started to change as she felt the positive thought energy that she had woken within her was healing her crippling fear of poverty and financial distress.

Within one month of using the invocation Jennie's life had started to blossom. Her fear of poverty had gone and she made decisions and choices which improved her life and made her financially better off. She paid off her debts, healed friendships and met a new lover.

After six months of doing the invocation Jennie began to realise a dream she had long held, to open her own school. Eventually, Jennie found the funding and set up her school, and her life is now richer in every way.

FEAR OF MONEY

The fear of money, which is closely linked to the fear of poverty, is about far more than money, which is simply the focus of the fear. It is about the fear of expressing your will, mind and emotions in order to take charge of your life. This can show itself in all sorts of ways. For instance by not paying bills, by allowing debts to mount up, by spending money you don't have, by allowing others to control your financial destiny without understanding what they are doing or by avoiding money issues or letting your mind go blank when money matters are to be discussed.

To overcome your fear of money is a major life experience. You will emerge into a state of higher consciousness and gain a practical understanding of your own personal power in the world. You will discover your own inner value while understanding the true value of money and you will allow success and prosperity into your life.

Use the Invocation for the Removal of Obstacles, outlined above, to address your fear of money.

CREATING WEALTH

People often hunt after money simply for the sake of having it. But they can do themselves damage, emotionally, physically and spiritually by doing this. Many people equate money with material power. But it is the thought energy that creates money that has the material power. You can use money thought energy to create situations that could make you rich. But this is an unskilful use of this energy and the cost to your integrity, humanity and self-knowledge can be great. Get-rich-quick schemes are emotionally and spiritually damaging when they are based on an unstable greed and a desire to own money. You cannot own money, just direct it well, and be a caretaker for the things that it buys you. If you treat money badly, it will rebound on you like a slap in the face. But understand it and treat it well and you will prosper.

These days people are often encouraged to visualise the amount of money they want, or to see money coming to them, to focus on becoming rich or to meditate on riches. In the Tibetan Bön view these actions are wrong. To focus on an amount of money you want is to take it from someone else in the world and is an action that will attract dark forces to you.

In the same way, to feel that you deserve money, for any reason at all, or to be grudging about money you have given up, lost or never had, will simply empower the obstacles preventing you from having money. No one deserves money, it is simply a question of having it or not having it, depending upon the nature of your thought energies.

The best way to bring money and wealth into your life is to begin by focusing on removing any obstacles that you have placed in the way of your own prosperity. The Removal of Obstacles Exercise above is valuable for this and so are the exercises that follow. By removing obstacles you open the way for new skilful thought energy to be created and for money and prosperity to come to you, in the appropriate form and amount.

Don had worked for twenty-seven years for a rail company, organising schedules and engineering works. At this point there were major changes in his company structure which Don didn't like. He was expected to take on new duties and he felt out of his depth. Don became depressed and after a few months he could no longer cope with work.

Don stayed at home for the next year, taking medication for his depression and hoping that his company would make him redundant and give him a payout. But while the company still paid him monthly, their policy was no redundancies, so Don didn't get his big cheque. This made Don more and more angry. He cursed his bosses and the company and thought non-stop about the money he felt he deserved for all his years of hard work.

When I met Don he wanted to know how he could make the company give him a big payout. I told him that he was going down the wrong route. First, he did not 'deserve' the money and thinking about it all the time was attracting negative energy to him. And second, to want money from people he disliked and was angry with was a big mistake. I explained that if he got the money he would attract a great deal of negativity with it, including all the hatred and anger he felt. Don was shaken by this because most people had told him to hang on for the money. But after thinking about it he decided to resign and forget about a payout. In his resignation letter he thanked the company for their generosity and support through his illness.

As soon as he had posted the letter Don began to feel relief surge through him. Within days his depression was lifting and three weeks later he had all his enthusiasm for life back and had decided to retrain as an osteopath. By letting go of his greed and anger Don had freed himself from the obstacles in his path and his health and wellbeing returned.

He also left himself free to attract prosperity, and a few years later Don was running a thriving practice and was earning more than he ever had at the rail company.

CREATING PROSPERITY

Prosperity is vitality born from the use of skilful thought energy, which attracts good circumstances to you. According to the ancient Tibetan Bön view it is possible to develop this important thought energy in order to create benefits for ourselves and for others. Bön teaching directs that there are six qualities that influence your relationship with yourself and the material world. They rise and fall with your inner tides of vitality, emotions, thoughts and life experience.

These six qualities are important to develop in ourselves and to balance with one another, if we are to direct skilful thought energy and create prosperity. Although they do not all appear to link directly with money, they are all equally relevant to creating skilful money thought energy, as money affects every aspect of ourselves.

This practice can be done to improve your general situation, for a specific reason or to attract good fortune into your life and create prosperity.

The Six Qualities

CHA

This expresses your destiny, or potential for making your life; it is the energy that you have brought into this life, the potential you have to work with. It is the underlying principle and force that expresses all positive aspects and dimensions of the other five qualities, mentioned below.

There is cha energy for every aspect of your mind, thoughts, activities and life. Thus, Cha is a pathway of energy that can lead you to an outcome. One of the many symbols that stands for Cha is pure, clean, clear water.

WANGTHANG

This represents prosperity, good fortune and personal power and relates to financial development. It is your ability to understand what needs to be improved upon or changed in your life and provides the energy and motivation for you to achieve your goals. A symbol for Wangthang is the grain barley.

LUNGTA

This is your protective energy, your inner knowledge and the amount of good fortune potential that you carry with you. Lungta expresses your abilities to be successful and helps you to know what types of success are best for you. One of the symbols for Lungta is a clear quartz crystal.

LÜ

This relates to the potential for your vitality and health and its influences upon your mental and physical health. One of the symbols for Lü is a small amount of fresh earth.

SOK

This expresses your life force, the deepest thought energy that runs through you and your life, the recurring theme that is unique to you. There are many symbols for Sok; one of them is a small amount of fresh butter.

LA

This is the essential energy of your life, the mother force that holds you up and keeps you going through life's ups and downs; it is the way thought energy translates itself from the cosmos into your human consciousness and daily life. A symbol for La is a small amount of ground plain salt.

When these last three qualities are weak or are declining due to unskilful thoughts, habits or illness then you are more likely to have low prosperity, poor vitality and feel that you cannot change your circumstances.

All six of these qualities need to be awakened and used to maintain and improve your ability to have prosperity and to understand it – especially in connection with money and its influence upon you.

How To Strengthen The Six Qualities

This is a simple but effective way to awaken these qualities within you and to strengthen them, as well as to bring you prosperity and bring about the success of any venture connected with abundance. The exercise is a little more complex than many of the others I have given, but is worth doing in the correct detail because it is powerful and effective. It is a simplified version of an ancient but very effective ritual that is safe and healing. Ensure than you have the necessary items ready and put aside a quiet hour in which to do it.

THE MEANING OF THE RITUAL

The water, barley, crystal, earth, butter and salt represent the six qualities. Clapping awakens dormant energies and alerts the gods to what you are asking for. Sprinkling water on your head is a symbol of purification.

Within Bön is a great body of stored knowledge, and rituals such as this one connect you to this reservoir of knowledge and awaken it within you.

Do the exercise once, if possible once a month on a full or a new moon. For very serious situations do it every three days. Alternatively, if you have an important opportunity, a meeting, a business venture or anything of importance, do it at sunrise and at sunset on the day before.

Draw a circle one foot in diameter, either on the earth or on a large thick piece of paper. Then draw another circle inside the first circle, two inches from the first. Divide the second circle into six equal sections. Number them one to six starting from the left-hand side.

In the first segment sprinkle a little clear water and say aloud, 'Cha!' In the second segment, sprinkle a little barley and say aloud, 'Wangthang!' In the third segment, place a little piece of clear quartz crystal, and say aloud, 'Lungta!' In the fourth segment, sprinkle a little fresh earth and say aloud, 'Lü!' In the fifth segment, place a little fresh butter and say aloud, 'Sok!' In the sixth segment, sprinkle a little salt and say aloud, 'La!'

When you have done this, clap your hands three times very loudly, and bow to each segment.

Then bow to each segment in the order that you sprinkled and say the following, speaking with strength and vigour: 'I summon and awaken my Cha. I summon and awaken my Wangthang. I summon and awaken my Lungta. I summon and awaken my Lü. I summon and awaken my Sok. I summon and awaken my La.'

As you do you this you start to activate these dormant thought forces within you, purifying your mind and body.

Now, standing up, sprinkle a little water on the top of your head, in the centre, and say, 'I purify my Cha.' Then clap your hands once.

Then gather up a little barley grain and sprinkle it over your shoulders, chest and heart area and as you do this say, 'I purify my Wangthang.'

Then placing a little piece of clear quartz crystal at your navel say, 'I purify my Lungta.'

Then gathering up a little earth sprinkle it over your feet or shoes while saying, 'I purify my Lü.'

Then taking up a little butter on the tip of your right index finger, smear it between your eyebrows moving up in a line to your hairline, saying, 'I purify my Sok.'

Then taking a little salt in each hand put your hands together as if you were washing, rubbing the salt over your hands, saying at the same time, 'I purify my La.'

When you have finished this, think of an aim or project to do with prosperity, money, or abundance. This does not mean a specific amount of money, but a goal connected with it, such as a new job, success in a work project or the repayment of debts. Write it down clearly and concisely in each segment of the circle. You can also say it aloud, and then with your left hand imagine that you have seized what you have said, and then you throw it down into each segment. For both methods think of this aim flowing into each area of your body that you have blessed with each of the six qualities and their substances.

Then stand or sit quietly contemplating what you have done. See each of your six qualities expanding out into the world, activating, stimulating and bringing about the aim you have thought about.

When you have finished, if you have drawn your circle on the earth then gently brush it away with your hands until it is dispersed. If you drew it on paper then set fire to the paper with all the things you have put on it, making sure to burn it safely.

Jade had wealthy parents and had been given a potentially easy life. Yet when she came to see me she was very distressed and in a terrible financial dilemma.

Her adult life had been far from easy and full of money problems. She was married, with a child, and both she and her husband were artists. Although they were both very talented, they had not found success and for some years her husband had been in a deep depression.

Jade herself felt no sense of happiness. They had lost all their money and had no sense of direction or ability to pull their lives together. Jade felt unhappy about her lifestyle and wanted to make changes and to learn how to make money and manage it well.

I taught Jade the balancing of the six qualities and almost immediately she began to make positive changes in her life.

Her husband saw these changes and decided to try it for himself. Gradually he emerged from his depression and found a new sense of energy and enthusiasm in his work.

Together Jade and her husband began to find success with their work. Their growing inner happiness and emotional prosperity led to material prosperity and they discovered a sense of balance and happiness together.

ATTRACTING MONEY

If you want to attract money then look first at your motives. These do not need to be spiritual or simply to benefit others, but they do need to be clear, honest and worthwhile. Watch out for greed, dishonesty or any other unskilful thought energy, which will drive money away from you rather than attracting it.

Use this five-point plan for creating directed and skilful thought energy, for attracting money and creating financial security.

---

1 Each day spend one hour focusing your thoughts on the nature, structure and quality of the type of financial success you want. You need to put a lot of time in at first to get this thought exercise up and running. Be specific about what it is you want to do and achieve.

2 Now identify the time in which you wish to achieve a certain goal or outcome. This could be five minutes, one day, a month, or a year.

3 Next send out a directed thought that clears any obstructions or problems that you may see or expect. Also direct thought energy to clear any form of obstructions or problems that you have not thought of. To help you do this effectively, imagine a column of fire is burning away problems, obstructions and difficult situations.

4 At this point send thought energy out into the world to attract good fortune and opportunities for advancement. Think that money now starts to flow to you, bringing peace and success and helping you to have a clear mind.
5 Now direct all the above thoughts together and imagine them merging, blending and becoming one powerful fiery ball of thought. Direct it out into the thought energies of all people and see it start to burn as a brilliant pure flame that creates wellbeing and attracts money to you immediately without harm to others.

After you feel comfortable with this thought direction exercise you can use it not just for planning results but for influencing outcomes in meetings, overcoming problems, achieving your goals, creating opportunities for success and turning negative situations into positive ones. If you use it responsibly it will work and bring results.

Daisy wanted to have a shop selling textiles, but she had no idea how to go about achieving this or raising the money for her shop.

Daisy realised that she had two great fears that stood in the way of her success: her fear of poverty and her fear of money, which was really a fear of being in control and achieving success. She had always felt very undeserving and her background, in which money was very tight, reinforced this.

For several weeks Daisy did the Removal of Obstacles Exercise and as her fears lifted she felt bolder and braver about her goals. She felt that removing these fears was a life-changing event and that all kinds of possibilities had opened up for her.

She moved on to the exercises to create prosperity and attract money and within six months she had found a backer, found a shop and created a good business plan.

Doing these exercises she learned a lot about her attitude to money and the way it influenced her life. As a result she found that all kinds of other areas of her life improved, including her health and relationships.

Daisy now has six shops and is very successful indeed. She uses this exercise each day as meditation tool for clear thought and skilful living. She also uses it as a powerful business tool to make decisions, overcome problems and to benefit her staff, suppliers and customers.

SHARING YOUR MONEY

In the Bön belief system when you share your money, you share yourself. If you do not share your money you lose your connection with it and with other people. Sharing what you have financially is the first step to developing compassion and tolerance for others less fortunate or able than you. Often by sharing our money we discover just how limited we have allowed ourselves to be and how powerful are the 'comfort zones' that we have created around ourselves through the use of money.

The sharing of money links people in good ways if it is shared well. Share with those whom you know will be grateful, not to please your ego, but so that the gift of money is received with care and appreciation.

SHARING MONEY THOUGHT EXERCISE

Do this exercise for ten minutes.

Sit comfortably. Close your eyes. Listen to your heartbeat and concentrate your mind and thoughts upon it.

Now consider all the money that you have, however much or little this is. Think of this amount merging with your heartbeat. As this happens see it flowing out into the world as thought energy bringing benefit to other people.

This exercise will connect you to others, through the money that you have and will help you to discover that you always have more than you realise and that there is always enough to share.

Tobin came from one of the richest families in the world. His life was one of privilege, comfort and financial security and yet he felt something was missing. One day one of his closest friends lost all his money. With it he lost his lifestyle and most of the friends who went with it. Except for Tobin.

Tobin wanted to help his friend but did not know how. He was afraid that to give his friend money might be wrong, as everyone around him told him it was.

When we met I taught Tobin the Tibetan Bön ideas about money and sharing. So he shared his money with his friend. His friend then rebuilt his life, paid Tobin back, and made a huge amount of money.

Together, Tobin and his friend now share their money with others, expecting nothing in return. They have helped many people rebuild their lives, start businesses and realise ambitions. They have also helped to create charities and inner city and rural regeneration programmes.

Tobin has never entered into paper contracts, but he did enter into contracts made up with skilful thinking. No one has ever cheated him.

When I last spoke to Tobin he said that he had come to understand, by sharing, that he was only a caretaker for the immense wealth he had inherited. He spends his time, to use his own words 'being of service to my fellow human beings'. Tobin has become rich in spirit due to his ability to share his good fortune.

GIVING THANKS

We live, for the most part, lives dominated by self-created routine and unskilful obligation. It is when we come upon moments of thankfulness that we become truly alive. Thankfulness is an immensely powerful skilful thought energy and this is why it is good to give thanks every day.

In giving thanks daily, we start to connect to the underlying forces of abundance. Give thanks not just for what you have, but also for what you do not have. Give thanks for all the good and the bad, the positive and the negative in your life. Give thanks, also, that you are free from the problems that others have. In this way you keep yourself free of these problems and you also lessen the misfortunes of others.

To give thanks is to open your heart. To open your heart is to experience what others experience. To experience what others experience is the first step in developing compassionate thought energy that can help others to be free of suffering and bring them happiness, wisdom and the power to create prosperity. Giving thanks teaches each of us the special responsibility that we have to use our personal and global resources wisely. Giving thanks reduces anger, transforms greed, and purifies lust, all of which are entwined in the structures of money.

THE GIVING THANKS THOUGHT EXERCISE

Giving thanks can help you to solve all your financial problems.

First make a list of all your problems with money. Then make a list of areas in your life where you have no problems with money. Then make lists of all the other good and bad things in your life. Now, speaking aloud, thank each thing in this way: 'I give thanks that I have a good job. I give thanks that my relationship broke up. I give thanks for my health. I give thanks for losing my money.'

Giving thanks heals the pain of the bad things and creates new opportunities for growth and financial success. It also secures and increases the power of the good things in every area of your life. Giving thanks brings peace, beauty and understanding to the skilful thought energy that lies behind all prosperity.

Above all give thanks for yourself, for who you are, have been, and shall be in the future.

BEFORE YOU GO

If you take money with you when you die, as thought energy which you are holding on to, then it may cause you and those who live after you unhappiness. According to Tibetan Bön teachings the thought energy of money can be passed down from one family member to another, through many generations. Make sure that you do not take with you, or pass on, the thought energy of greed, selfishness or meanness.

It is very important that, before you die, you put your affairs in order and make sure that your money and assets will go to those you have chosen. Freeing yourself of your financial connections before you die will create a lightness in your being and will help you to achieve a peaceful death.

5

ENHANCING YOUR RELATIONSHIPS

Relationships are the foundation of humanity. We derive our nourishment from them, learn from them and thrive through them. Every human being wants to relate to other human beings; it is an essential part of who we are as individuals and as a species. And the way in which we relate to others determines how happy we are, how long we live and the choices we make. Through our relationships we discover our place in the world and our reason for being here.

For these reasons it is very important that we share ourselves with others in ways that feel right and good. Unhappy relationships, loneliness and hatred all damage our sense of self and of our rightful place in the world.

Each one of us has many different kinds of relationships. We have partners, children, families, friends, work colleagues, and more incidental relationships with people we meet in shops and even those we listen to on the radio or watch on TV. Even when we want nothing to do with someone, or avoid them, we still have a relationship with them. So the way we conduct these relationships, whether close, casual or distant, is vital.

In the Bön view relationships are based on shared thought energy. The more powerful the relationship – whether this be through love or hate – the stronger the thought energy shared between the two people concerned. The key to relationships is the development of one's own thought energy, because in this way we learn to relate more skilfully and to recognise the quality of thought energy directed towards us from others. With skilful thought energy we learn to use good judgement in choosing who we want to relate to and we learn to manage and deepen the relationships we want to focus on. In other words, the nature of our relationships is based on the way we think.

In the next chapter I will look at specific family relationships, including husbands, wives, children, parents and siblings. I will explain how to attract and to develop a love relationship with a potential partner and how to use the power of sexual energy in positive ways.

But first, in this chapter I will look at the nature of friendship. The thread of friendship runs through all forms of relationship because it is about the search for intimacy between two people. Before there were civilisations, when humankind was in its infancy, there was friendship. Friendship is based on the oldest and most intrinsic human awareness that there is more to life than just ourselves. In this chapter I will explain the essence of friendship and how you can bring the kinds of friends and relationships you want into your life. I will also explain how to heal relationships that have gone wrong, how to let go of those that need to move on and how to deepen the inner relationship you have with yourself.

THE THOUGHT ENERGY OF RELATIONSHIPS

Ancient Tibetan wisdom sees a friend as someone who is linked to you, whether for a moment or a lifetime, by the same desire for spiritual awareness. This link is forged by the power of thought energy. The thought energy of relationships begins and ends with the way each of us thinks. Our minds are storehouses of power and this power comes from the different types of thought energy that we have. Each thought we have makes a structure within us. Think of it as a battery, with a lifespan and a power source of its own.

Our individual thought energy seeks out communication with other people, so that it can replicate itself in others and thus create a powerful interaction of thought energy. Our thoughts are messengers carrying our desires into the minds of others. Thought energy has being doing this for countless aeons, since long before humanity arrived on the earth. So when people of like minds meet up, their thought energy connects, creating a powerful and dynamic force. Think of a time when you have met someone and felt you knew them already, or a time when you spotted someone across a room and felt strongly drawn to them, as a friend or as a lover. This is thought energy at its most powerful. At other times the connection is not as immediately apparent; it takes longer to make the link, yet it may last for many years and be extremely strong.

The life of a relationship is determined at its outset by the union of thought energy that is created between the participants. A relationship may last a day or a lifetime, it may be superficial or powerfully deep, according to the thought energy connection created at its beginning. This is also true for events, movements, countries and cultures, for all of them are dependent on the relationships at their core. If a great artistic movement lasts for only a few years, if religions and cultures last for several millennia, if an national event lasts for a day, all of them depend on the thought energy that was created at their beginning.

YOUR RELATIONSHIP WITH YOURSELF

Learning to think well, with care, compassion, integrity and structure, can be our greatest gift to the body of humanity, as well as to ourselves. If we want to have satisfying, happy and creative relationships, we must first begin by getting to know and understand our own inner thought processes.

One of the best ways to do this is to create a connection with your own Inner Friend, the wise, loving and loyal part of yourself which is always waiting to befriend you as well as others. Your Inner Friend is in harmony with everyone and with all living creatures. He or she gets on with anyone from any walk of life and knows that the value and importance of friendship comes from the skill of the thought energy that brings people together.

By tuning in to the thought energy of your Inner Friend, you can learn how to establish strong and secure relationships, heal rifts in existing relationships and see more clearly which relationships are of value to you and which are not. You will also learn from your Inner Friend what kind of friend you are and have the potential to be and why you have the friends that you do.

Above all your Inner Friend is there for you. No matter what is happening in your life or in the world around you, your Inner Friend will guide, support and love you.

Invoking your Inner Friend

Arrange in front of you a clean bowl of water, a piece of self-lighting charcoal in a bowl, and either a bottle of juniper essential oil or a few juniper berries. Light the charcoal and once it is lit either place the juniper berries on the charcoal or sprinkle on a little essential oil. Then, after cleaning your hands, sprinkle a little of the water on your head, face and in the area where you are sitting. Imagine a circle of juniper smoke surrounding you so that you are in the circle's centre. The juniper will purify your environment, remove thought obstructions and stimulate and awaken skilful thought energies. The water also purifies, dissolves obstructions and balances the environment.

Sit quietly. Be aware of your breathing. Close your eyes and allow yourself to relax. Now imagine that you are seeing within yourself. Stay in this inner place. Then call for your Inner Friend to appear.

You do it like this: *'I call out, here in this sacred place, to my Inner Friend, come forth!'*

Be completely open to whatever will appear. Your Inner Friend may appear either as a man or a woman, clothed or naked, young or old, or also as completely neutral – neither male nor female, ageless, eternal. As your Inner Friend appears do not be in a hurry or over-excited, just receive the presence of your Inner Friend. Be thankful, be humble.

You now need to gain the attention of your Inner Friend, by saying your name, quietly out loud. For example: 'My name is Dave,' or 'My name is Cathy.'

At this point your Inner Friend will look at you. Be ready to ask a question about problems or issues in your life. You will get an answer. You can ask your Inner Friend questions about friendship, friends that you have or yourself as a friend. Always ask your questions aloud, quietly and clearly.

When you feel that you have had enough it is time to thank your Inner Friend and ask if you can meet again. You must do this in the traditional Bön way, using the Inner Friend's Tibetan name, Phug Lha, which is that of a group of Tibetan Bön deities or angels who look after the home, family and friends.

'I thank you, Phug Lha, for answering all that I have asked. I ask that soon we shall meet again.'

Then slowly open your eyes, clap your hands three times very loudly (this arouses your energy and invites the gods to pay attention to what you have done) and sprinkle your head, face and sitting area with water. Place a little juniper, oil or berries on the charcoal and imagine the circle of juniper smoke around you fading away.

Diana was an extremely unhappy woman who came to me for help with medical problems. Underneath these problems lay her deep insecurity and lack of belief in herself. Because of this Diana held herself back in relationships and refused to trust another person. Diana was a successful business-woman with a beautiful home and many possessions. She appeared glamorous and many envied her lifestyle. She appeared to have it all, but felt that she had very little. She had reached the age of fifty-seven still living alone, with many acquaintances but no partner or children and no true friends.

I encouraged Diana to do this exercise, invoking her own Inner Friend. At first she was reluctant, but she knew that change must start from within, so she agreed to do it for one month.

After a month Diana came back to tell me that she had discovered a wonderful Inner Friend, a loving and wise woman who gave her warmth and guidance. She had asked her Inner Friend why she always resisted becoming close to anyone and her friend had told her that this was a behaviour she had developed in childhood as a means of self-protection. Diana had lost both her parents when she was five and had become afraid to let anyone close again, for fear of losing them. Her friend told her that she no longer needed this self-protection and that, as an adult, she could make wise judgements about who to be close to.

Diana was delighted and glowed with new-found energy. Two months later she told me that she was beginning to make deeper and more satisfying friendships. Best of all, a male friend she had always liked had become much closer to her and she had fallen in love with him. He had always cared for her, but she had not realised this, or let him come close, until now. Diana was amazed by this, and also by her own wisdom, revealed though her Inner Friend.

THE THIRD PERSON

From the Tibetan view we are responsible for our relationships because we create them and give them life and influence over us. When two people connect through their joint union of thought energies the relationship they create exists as a separate body of thought energy, connected to both people by their common links, emotions and thought.

In order to enable a relationship to continue, this 'Third Person', as it is called in the Bön teachings, needs to be cared for and kept healthy. This is done in two ways. First through the quality of thought energy that travels between the people in the relationship, and second by focusing specifically on the Third Person itself. Each person in the relationship needs to spend a few minutes, every now and then, directing positive thoughts into the Third Person.

The Third Person takes on all the qualities of each person involved and can exist between individuals, groups, businesses and nations. As long as there is a vital connection between two or more people the Third Person exists, gaining strength and vitality.

However, people often forget that a relationship needs work, and if the Third Person is not cared for it will begin to fade and eventually the relationship will die. When this happens the people in the relationship lose vitality. They become less, for a while, than they were. This is why separations can cause so much pain and heartache.

THOUGHT ENERGY EXERCISE FOR NOURISHING THE THIRD PERSON

This exercise will help you to nourish and enrich the Third Person between you and anyone you share a relationship with. This can be a partner, lover, relative or friend, a business colleague or someone you would like to know better.

Sit quietly in any way that feels comfortable and be as relaxed as you can. Close your eyes. Start to listen to any sounds around you, in your immediate environment. Turn your attention now to your body and listen to the sounds of your body. After a few minutes move your attention to your mind and listen to the sounds there.

As you listen, let the inner noise of your mind come and go, and when you're ready, start to focus your attention upon the person you have a relationship with. Listen to their environment, if you know where they are. Listen to their body and then listen to their mind.

After doing this for as long as you want, focus your attention upon the Third Person. You will very quickly sense this person and begin to notice the form it takes. It may be male or female, young or old, wise or innocent. This form is showing you the true nature of your relationship.

In order to nurture the Third Person, simply spend a few minutes with it, getting to know it and focusing positive thought energy on it.

Guide to Interpreting the Form of your Third Person

MALE

If your Third Person comes in male form, it shows that your relationship is governed by male principles and energies and by male thought energy.

FEMALE

If your Third Person appears in female form, then your relationship is governed by female principles and energies, and by female thought energy.

WISE

This form indicates that there is wisdom in the relationship that needs to be listened to by both parties and then put into action in the everyday world.

INEXPERIENCED

If your Third Person appears to be adult but naïve and inexperienced, it shows that both parties have not spent enough time giving life to the relationship and merely react to each other, rather than interact. This relationship is surviving but not thriving, and needs to be developed to a deeper level.

IMBALANCED

A Third Person who you sense is out of balance shows too many other influences are affecting the growth of the relationship; past baggage and worries of the moment are affecting the stability of this relationship and need to be dealt with so that the relationship can thrive.

BABY

This reveals that the relationship is only in its infancy, regardless of how it may appear to each partner and to the outside world.

CHILD

Curiosity, communication and a delight for each other's presence are important in this relationship. However, growth and guidance are needed and both partners need to share their feelings and hopes for the future.

TEENAGER

Rebellion, questioning, looking for meaning, exploring the boundaries, trying to make sense of things are all issues in this relationship. What it needs to create balance is patience, understanding and tolerance. It needs to move from a love/hate experience to a love/love experience. Let the Third Person grow up into a balanced, mature and successful adult.

ADULT

This Third Person has started to be developed and nurtured and therefore returns blessings to the partnership. An adult Third Person can normally survive the challenges of life. Mutual understanding has arrived.

OLD PERSON

Integrated, harmonious, tolerant and complete. This Third Person is very well looked after and so naturally is part of the flow of thought energy in this balanced and successful relationship.

To the outside world James and his girlfriend Francesca seemed to be happy and stable. But deep down inside James felt that there was something missing in the relationship; he wanted better communication with the woman he loved, and yet he didn't know how to do this. He and his girlfriend were arguing a lot, sometimes violently, accused each other of keeping secrets and had long periods of refusing to talk to each other.

By the time he came to see me James was feeling very isolated and he told me that his girlfriend was becoming more and more withdrawn. I asked James to do the Third Person exercise and to tell me what he found.

When he returned he said that the Third Person had been a teenage boy, very bright, curious and fun but also very angry and rebellious. I explained to him that this teenager, who represented James and Francesca's relationship, needed to grow up. For this he needed patience, tolerance and understanding, along with firm, loving boundaries.

James began to put this into action, setting boundaries by refusing to row with Francesca and instead approaching the relationship with patience and understanding.

James told me that over the next few weeks Francesca began to soften and to be more open with him about her past. She had been afraid that James wouldn't love her if he knew that she had been out with a lot of men before she met him. As James offered her loving acceptance the two of them grew closer.

Six months later James reported that the Third Person had now become a mature young adult, able to handle the ups and downs of the relationship without tears and tantrums. James had told Francesca about the exercise and they now did it together every week.

THE MEANING AND VALUE OF RELATIONSHIPS IN YOUR LIFE

When you are satisfied in your relationships then you will be satisfied with your life as a whole. Looking at the relationships in your life, the number, the quality, the level of contact you have, will give you a clear indication of what is wrong or right with your life in general and which areas will benefit from development. Think about the following questions and see how many are true for you.

Are your relationships hurried and often brief?
Do you squeeze friends and family in when you have a spare moment?
Do you treat friends selfishly, only calling them when you have a need? Are friends just people you get on well with?

Do you refuse to let anyone get too close to you?
Are you often suspicious of people who seem to like you?
Are you often thoughtless and uncaring towards your friends?
Do you ever end friendships abruptly because someone has offended you?
Do you make a new friend on the basis of what you will get from them?
Are you reluctant to say sorry when you have hurt someone?

If you answered yes to any of these questions then it will give you useful information about the areas of skilful thought energy that you need to develop. True friendships involve trust, loyalty, depth and compassion. They always work two ways; a friendship out of balance will not last. Friendship is a way to grow up, share who you are, and become a better person. Friendships teach you how to think, feel, act and make decisions. It is in friendship that you discover your humanity and the ability for compassion and love.

FRIENDSHIP TYPES

Not all friendships are the same. It wouldn't be possible to make all your friendships lasting and deep, but neither do you want them all to be brief and superficial. The chances are that your friendships fall into one of these three major types:

FIVE-MINUTE WONDERS

These are people who enter your life for a brief time and bring you positive change and new ideas, before moving on. They are often valuable and leave a lasting mark, even though you may not know them for long. Never feel regret about such people; they are not meant to be in your life for long.

CONSUMERS

These are the people who can often seem wonderful at first, but who leave you feeling drained and exhausted every time you see them. This is because they are takers and will tend to focus their energy and yours on themselves. They may do this charmingly, so that it takes a while to spot what's going on. People who are used to caring for others, or who are not sure of themselves in friendships tend to attract consumers. But the relationships don't last because when the consumer has exhausted you enough you will begin to avoid them.

OLD FAITHFULS

These are people who come into your life and stay. Friendships with old faithfuls are genuine and deep, they mature slowly and give you rich nourishment, spiritually and emotionally. With these people you know you can be yourself, be totally open and honest and feel loved and supported. These friendships are balanced, over the long term; a friend may help you through a crisis and then, perhaps much later, you will help them in return. Such friendships are extremely valuable and need to be cared for and fed. You will never have more than a small handful of this kind of relationship because this level of intimacy is not possible with more than a few people during a lifetime.

Look at your own friendships and see which categories they come into. Ideally you will have a few old faithfuls, a larger scattering of five-minute wonders and the occasional passing consumer.

How to Deepen Your Friendships

This exercise will help you to create deeper friendships with people you already know. Perhaps you would like someone you have recently met to become a lasting friend, or perhaps a long-term friendship needs new energy to keep it going and thriving.

Creating an extra dimension or a new level of experience to your friendships will also help you to deepen your relationships with your partner, children, parents and other family members.

These three guidelines on how to communicate with your friends in order to improve the friendship are taken from very ancient Bön tribal teachings.

- Anyone can speak aloud. This is not the way. Speak from your heart and do it simply. Back up your words with actions.
- Listen with care to every word a person speaks – you can hear the quality of their soul. Do their words and soul agree?
- Be silent and calm in all responses. Be happy and loving. Direct your answers to the centre of the person you speak with. Let the power within you guide your words and thoughts.

These three points are essential in knowing the hearts of our friends and our own hearts as well. Such skilled communication unites people in courage and powerful connection.

The Skilful Relationships Thought Exercise

This thought energy exercise teaches you how to cultivate skilful friendship and how to deepen and strengthen friendships. The art of creating skilful relationships comes from understanding how you think about them and what you want from them. Relationships need nourishment to thrive and this nourishment comes from skilful thought energy. As you examine thought energy in this way, your intuitive powers will suddenly blossom.

Do this exercise each morning before breakfast for one month. It should take about twenty minutes to complete.

Sit in a comfortable chair with your feet a little apart; don't cross your legs and let your palms rest in your lap. Close your eyes and focus on your breathing. Now imagine that you can hear a drum beating, slowly but with force. As the drum beats, you see a spiral of red light; a net of red light is being built around you, a protective net, a net made up of your thought energy.

Now think of the person with whom you would like a deeper friendship and think about the kind of relationship you want to create. Place your thoughts into the net.

When you are ready, imagine that you are gathering this net up and casting it high into the sky. See it blown by powerful winds and falling upon the person concerned. This causes them no harm and if this relationship is meant to be then this will draw the person to you and allow for a deeper, more meaningful relationship.

Bridget was Miss Popularity. She had been queen of her school ball and had always been surrounded by friends and people who wanted to know her. Ten years later it dawned on her that she really didn't know anything about any of her many friends. Her life was a social whirl, yet she felt hollow, washed up and tired and became quite depressed.

Bridget came to see me about her depression and as we talked she realised that she had spread her energy too wide, trying to be friends with everyone and accepting every invitation. She had never developed the handful of close, personal friendships that are essential in a balanced life.

Bridget began the thought exercise for creating skilful friendships. She did this exercise every morning for a month, concentrating on two people she really wanted to know better. After a month both these people, quite separately, began to offer her a deeper quality of friendship. One of them asked for her help with a project, while the other asked her to come on a holiday. Bridget gladly accepted and put her energy into strengthening and deepening these friendships.

As time went on Bridget found that she was able to let a lot of her more superficial friendships go; there simply wasn't room for them in her life, now that she was spending more time with her two special friends.

As she made these adjustments in her life Bridget found her depression lifting and her sense of purpose returning. She felt more centred and mature. She had come to understand that trying to be friends with everyone, all the time, is simply a way of resisting being truly close to anyone.

CREATING FRIENDSHIPS

In any human activity that involves others we seek the intimacy of friendship. We want to share connections with others and to communicate our inner truths. To some people friendship comes easily, but for others it is much harder to make and keep friends. Painful shyness, fear of rejection, feeling socially awkward and lack of confidence can all lead to loneliness and lack of friends, or to rejection by those you would like to be friends with.

Yet by cultivating the skilful thought energy of friendship you can draw friends into your life, no matter how difficult you have found this in the past. Changing the way you think about friendship will change your friendship pattern. As you see yourself become someone who is able to be a true friend and who has a great deal to offer in friendship, so you will attract those who also have genuine friendship to offer.

Right now in every city, in every neighbourhood, every place in the world where there are people, there is someone who would like to be your friend. You just haven't met them yet. This thought energy exercise will bring friends into your life.

THE FISHING FOR FRIENDS THOUGHT EXERCISE

Close your eyes and imagine a huge and fast-flowing river of human thought energy. You are standing on the riverbank and all you can see is light bouncing off its smooth and powerful surface. You can sense that something is going on beneath the surface, but you can't see it.

At this point, with a focused mind and direct thought, cast a fishing line far out into the middle of the river, see it splash and sink, the hook going beneath the surface. Now send all your wishes, longings and desires for friends down your fishing line into the hook, where the thought energy will sit, like bait, attracting bites in the form of other people's thought energy.

As you focus upon this you will begin to feel responses. Let the responses come, but don't rush. Take your time and begin gently to reel in your line and the friendship energy you have attracted. Feel this energy travelling along your line and into your heart.

LANDING THE CATCH

Within ten days, or even less, people will start to come into your life wanting to be friends. Make sure that you recognise all the opportunities for friendship that you have attracted to yourself. All types of people will come into your life so use your discretion and inner wisdom to choose those who will be the right friends for you. From time to time you will come across a few catches that must be thrown back. Among all the good and pleasant people you will find one who may be trouble. This happens as a test of your own inner balance and integrity and all you need to do is to let this person pass by and move on to others.

Herb lived in New York and ran his family business. He had plenty of family, but no friends, and although he longed to make friends he had no idea how. He had been brought up by very domineering parents and had never been encouraged to go out and make friends or to bring friends to the family home.

Herb had very little confidence, and thought everyone else was smarter, more attractive and more interesting than he was. He worked very hard and felt he had very few opportunities for making friends, and when there was an opportunity he usually blew it by running a mile.

I taught Herb how to do the Fishing for Friends Thought Exercise and as soon as he did it he felt a little more confident. He continued to do the exercise every day and in sending out thought energy he focused on what he had to offer and realised that he had lots of friendship potential.

Within days Herb started to reel in potential new friends. He met people in stores, at bus stops, at the gym and in all sorts of places where he had never imagined meeting friends. Neighbours began to chat to him and as people approached him he plucked up the courage to chat back and to ask to meet them again.

A year later I met Herb again and he was a changed man. The address book he'd never even bothered to use before was filled with names and numbers. He had a busy social life and had cut back on his working hours. Best of all he had met a lovely girl and got engaged.

BUILDING FRIENDSHIPS

Connecting your thought energy with potential friends is an act of skilful thinking. For this connection to mature into a fully fledged friendship, you need to choose the right moment for things to happen. According to Bön wisdom these are the best times in the day to attract friendship because at these times people are more open to the specific type of friendship:

- 11 a.m. until midday for all types of long-standing friendships that will be honest, communicative and rewarding.
- 12 noon until 3 p.m. for friendships involving a similar job, vocation, or calling.
- 5 p.m. until 8 p.m. for opportunities for platonic relationships between the sexes.
- 9 p.m. until midnight for long-term sexual and romantic liaisons and relationships.
- 1 a.m. until 3 a.m. for enduring friendships and/or relationships.
- 5 a.m. until 7 a.m. for creative and artistic friendships.
- 7 a.m. until 11 a.m. for family and financial bonds.

It is between these hours that your connections with the type of friendships mentioned have their best chance of instigation and success. Use these times for meetings, phone calls and letters which will deepen the kinds of connections you want. Obviously the middle of the night is not always an ideal time to call a friend, but you can also use these times to think about the person you have in mind, or write to them.

Any unspecified times are not constructive to developing meaningful friendships.

LONELINESS

The ancient Bön practitioners considered that someone who felt isolated or lonely had not been able to develop fully and become an adult because they could not feel at peace with their family line. If there was bad feeling or a dispute between that person and a parent, grandparent or other relative, or even a history of dispute which was affecting the person, then they would have no spiritual energy inside them from the family line and would be unable to become a complete adult.

If you are suffering from feelings of isolation or loneliness then you need to make peace with your family line, both maternal and paternal, and to forgive any pain that has been caused, no matter how far back along the line this was.

Roseanne had all her life felt separate from other people. Although she had a successful career in showbusiness and plenty of friends, her life felt very empty. When she came to see me, she told me that deep inside she was very lonely, and had always felt like this. She had found it impossible to connect deeply with others and only really felt comfortable on her own, although socially she behaved like the life and soul of the party.

When I asked about her family Roseanne tossed her head and told me that she hadn't spoken to her parents for ten years. She blamed them for her unhappy childhood and felt that they didn't really love her or want her to be happy. She was also distant from her brother and sister, although she had some contact with them.

I asked Roseanne to sit quietly for ten minutes each morning and concentrate on her family line, making peace with her parents and forgiving them for any past hurts. Roseanne reluctantly agreed to do this.

Two weeks later she returned to tell me that as she had done the exercise for the first time she had found herself weeping and had felt the most immense sense of relief. Something she had decided was unimportant – her damaged relationship with her parents – was in fact so important that it was blocking her life from moving forward.

A month later Roseanne told me that she had written to her parents suggesting she visit them and they had called her, delighted. She had spent a weekend with them and had found a new, calmer and more loving way of being with them. Within a year of this Roseanne told me that her sense of loneliness had disappeared, her friendships had deepened and she had begun a relationship with a man she loved.

THE FAMILY LINE EXERCISE

Sit quietly for a few minutes and focus on both your family lines, the one going back through your mother and the one going back through your father. It doesn't matter whether you know your true parents or not, you can still focus your mind on them and the families who came before them. Focus on drawing strength into you from these endless lines of ancestors and attaching yourself to the strongest forces of your family.

When you do this you will no longer feel isolated; the strength and love of your family, going back through generations, will always be with you.

Creating A Friendship with Someone Who Doesn't Like You

In some situations, for instance at work or in your neighbourhood you may regularly have contact with someone you feel doesn't like you and you may feel that the best solution is to make a friend of them.

The best and most effective way to create a friendship is to start from the following five points:

- Consider whether you have caused the person to dislike you. After having assessed this either way, direct a gentle stream of loving thought energy to this person.
- Then direct this love to you, washing away any real or imaginary prejudice that you may have towards this person. You will start to see them in a new light.
- Make peace with others who support the individual's dislike of you. Send them loving and uplifting thought energy. Bless them with thoughts of happiness.
- Remove all obstacles from the past, present and future with thought energy.
- Be prepared to take time over this. To do it well is based upon crafting your thought energy so that the person concerned comes to you. Then you have permission to express your desire for friendship.

This approach not only works but creates long and lasting positive friendships. Be patient, the first step may simply be that the two of you begin to talk. Stick with it and success will be yours.

HEALING RELATIONSHIPS

When relationships go wrong it can be very painful for one or both of the people concerned. If hatred, anger and enmity have entered a relationship then they need to be resolved and healed. This is true even if the people involved are no longer in contact. As long as they have strong negative feelings for one another then the relationship is not over and will have a profound and damaging effect on both of them.

To be an enemy is to have a most intimate relationship, for you are focusing huge amounts of thought energy on a particular person.

The nature of the thought energy of enemies and enmity binds people together in many unseen ways and will destroy your vitality, happiness and personal integrity. Being an enemy will also create ill health in both the person sending and the person receiving the negative thought energy.

For this reason it is important to understand the underlying nature of why we fall out and become enemies and to resolve and heal enmity.

The Bön teachers believed that there are nine possible causes:

Anger

This is the language of being an enemy; it is the thought energy that we fire, like invisible ammunition, on to the person who we regard as an enemy. In this situation, anger blinds your inner self to the possibilities of finding other ways to heal the situation.

Healing Anger

This exercise will heal anger, whether it is coming from you or being directed towards you. If you are the angry one you must be brave and rise above what you feel. Do this at least three times a week, first thing in the morning, because it is better to start your day in a state of compassion that in one of confusion.

First sit quietly and close your eyes. Focus your mind upon your heart and there in your heart see the person or situation causing or sending you anger. As you focus on this see your heart begin to glow with a soft pink light and the light slowly grow in intensity.

As this light deepens your insight into this problem grows until suddenly your physical heart bursts into flames. The fire burns all the anger away. It burns until the anger is gone and as it stops all that is left is a soft abiding peace filled with compassion and intelligence which guides you to solutions.

Direct this compassion towards the person who is regarding you as an enemy or whom you regard as an enemy.

Greed

The greed we have towards the enemy comes when we try to control them and wish to own what they think, feel or do. It is the origin of unchecked rivalry between individuals, institutions, corporations, nations, ideologies and religion and is based on a desire to see them admit that you are right and they are wrong. Greed is 'us and them' and is very divisive.

Healing Greed

Do this every day, before bed, for at least ten minutes.

Close your eyes, place your hands in your lap, palms up, and focus on your breathing. See this greed thought energy flowing out of your body, your mind and your soul and out of your life and all your points of reference.

Lust

This is the desire to have what others have, even their pain. Lust seeks to involve itself in what it cannot have and has no right to. Lust is different to greed in that it does not have a plan but is senseless in its desire to obtain. Thought energy is easily polluted by lust and it can be passed on to other people, making them suffer too.

Healing Lust

This simple meditation will heal the effects of lust you may feel for, or receive from, an enemy. Do this each morning for ten minutes until such time as you see or feel a change.

Sit quietly. Close your eyes. Place your concentration into the crown of your head and there imagine a gentle fountain is bubbling and flowing over you, cascading and cleansing you of this lust thought energy. The water that comes from this foundation is not ordinary water but a flowing and living light, sparkling with translucence and clarity, silver in colour and as it flows over you it has the sound of gentle wind chimes.

Money Issues

Often money and the problems generated in connection with money cause enemies to be created. Money contains within its thought energy powerful emotions and can lead to enmity when people identify too closely with it.

Healing Money Issues

Do this before bed for ten or fifteen minutes once a week, or more if you feel you need to.

As you sit quietly, close your eyes and in your mind visualise the enemy you have made due to money. See this person being showered in a soft rain of gold. The gold washes over them, healing their problems while at the same time making them feel rich and supported, with their own inner sense of contentment.

Love

Love can create enemies when the offer of love is rejected, or when the ending of a love relationship causes pain and anger. It can also cause problems when a lover is over-controlling or demanding. Love can cause enmity in all kinds of love relationships, between partners, family members or friends.

Healing Love Enmity

Do this at any time for as long as you can.

Sit still and quietly. Put your concentration into your heart. Focus on your heartbeat, and then slowly give up all the painful situations that have caused this enmity. Give it all away, and as you do you will discover that a more skilful love naturally takes its place.

Trust

Trust is the fragile bond created when two people's thought energies merge as one and find mutual support and recognition. When this is broken, one half of this mutual trust grieves for the loss of the other half and enemies can be created.

Healing Broken Trust

Do this for at least ten minutes, first thing each morning, for one month.

After you wake up, be still. Focus upon the person involved in this situation and see the trust becoming whole again. See the pain and confusion being cast away as understanding and forgiveness heal the hurt.

Power

When people share power and one loses it, the shock of this loss is as powerful as the death of someone close to you. This loss of connection with the shared experience of power can create hate and despair, for people believe that power solves inner shortcomings or that it somehow makes life better and can feel helpless without it.

Healing Power Enmity

Do this for ten minutes each day for one month.

Each morning on waking focus upon the top of your head. Visualise a great downward flow of brilliant golden light, inside and outside you, removing all the obstacles created by the unskilful thought energy of power.

As you feel this energy flow down within your body, stretch out your arms, hands and fingers, then direct this golden light out through your hands to the person who has become your enemy. See every obstacle melt away. Divine and spiritual power replaces all obstacles and peace and contentment flow to everyone.

Friendship

When we lose a friend through an argument, through jealousy or by a breach of trust, we create for ourselves a quandary. Do we choose to be kind and forgive or to be vindictive and become an enemy?

It takes maturity truly to forgive and forget; negative reactions are far easier as they come from your everyday mind, the mind and thought energy that merely reacts to things and has not yet forged a deep connection to the inner resources of consciousness.

When a friendship breaks down this is an opportunity to learn about the nature of friendship, even if the friendship cannot be salvaged.

Healing Friendship Enmity

Do this for ten minutes every morning for a month.

Sit quietly and picture the person concerned in your mind. See them dissolving in front of you and once they have totally dissolved, breathe in and then out and see them re-forming again, perfect and brand-new in mind and body. In this way you will see that the opportunity for healing this situation is ready to be seized.

Donald and Martin had known one another and been great friends since they were teenagers. When they left college they set up an advertising company together, which was very successful.

They made lots of money and enjoyed their success, and their friendship, until they both fell in love with the same woman. She went out with both of them, but in the end Donald got the girl and married her. Martin was terribly jealous and a few months later he accused Donald of dishonest dealing over company finances. They decided to split and to sell the company, but got into a huge legal mess. They both racked up enormous lawyers' bills, while refusing even to speak to one another.

A year later Martin came to see me about his lifestyle, which he felt was exhausting him. As we looked at different aspects of his life he realised how much he missed Donald.

Martin began the exercise for healing friendship enmity. He did this every day for six weeks and felt all his anger, bitterness and hurt towards Donald dissolving as his love for his friend resurfaced. Martin called Donald and asked to meet. Donald was naturally cautious; they had only spoken through lawyers for a year. But he agreed and the two men met for a drink.

Martin apologised to Donald for his jealousy and told his friend how much he had missed him. Donald was deeply touched and said he had missed Martin too. He also told Martin that his wife had left him, taking a huge financial settlement with her.

The two friends sold their agency and spent the proceeds on a small bar and grill in a tropical hideaway. They had a fantastic time running it and two years later they met sisters, whom they fell for and married. These days Donald and Martin never take their friendship for granted. They treat each other with appreciation and respect. By losing what they had they learned the true value of it.

Ownership

Ownership is often the cause of enmity. If people are jealous of one another's success, happiness, partners, children or possessions then this can lead to hatred.

But if you try to own something, whether a person or an object, an idea or a belief, when there is no underlying thought energy that connects you with it you cannot succeed. When people attempt to own what is not theirs it will lead to unhappiness and illness.

Healing Ownership Problems

Do this daily for ten minutes, until the situation changes.

Stand up, relaxed and quiet. Close your eyes and start to let go of any claims to ownership that you have made. As you do this you will feel immense spiritual power. Direct this power to the person involved and all the unskilful power thought energy that has caused you to be enemies will dissolve. All negative ownership energy is washed away, bringing innocence and harmony into the hearts of all involved.

RELATIONSHIP ENDINGS

All things have an end and we will all experience many relationship endings during our lives. Sometimes these are straightforward, the relationship feels complete and we are able to move on quickly and to come to terms with the ending easily.

At other times the endings can be messy, painful, drawn-out or bewildering. In these instances it is a great help to be able to understand what has happened and to create an ending that feels more complete. This will also help to create better relationships for the future, where thought energies collide with opportunities and become new relationships.

When close friendships come to an end it is because the lessons that you both needed to learn have been learned and it is time for both of you to move on. You both are needed elsewhere. If that is meant to be, you will meet each other again in some different guise. The wisdom and love from your friendship can be shared with others who need to learn the lessons that you have learned. Friendships, like thoughts, do not really die, they merely change their form.

So when a friend has moved on, even if the way it has happened is painful, do not hold them back. Let them go with your blessings and accept that your friendship has helped another fellow human being to find the next step in their life's journey.

Hurt and Betrayal

When a relationship ends through betrayal of any kind, you may feel let down, angry, used or humiliated. You may also feel profoundly hurt and unable to make sense of it all.

In Bön wisdom when a friend betrays you, they betray themselves. When you feel bewildered, your friend is bewildered even if it is not obvious. When you are hurt, so is your friend. In all these intense experiences your friendship is still alive, but has changed its quality and shape. You are sharing different things, most of which may cause you to part company.

At this point you need to decide whether to end the relationship or revive it with a new form and structure. This is possible, but it is hard to do; you have to be sure about the person and know who they really are.

Betrayal, bewilderment and hurt can all be healed, because healing is the natural process of life and of thought energy. So if a friend has ever betrayed you, you can become complete again and realise that you didn't lose a friendship, it merely changed its course, and from it you gained wisdom, understanding and discernment.

THE ETERNAL RELATIONSHIP

Although we can prosper, grow, learn and be happy through our relationships with other people we must also learn to do this with ourselves. Within us is the potential to have an eternal relationship with the divinity, spirituality and knowledge within. This comes about when we make contact with the inner kernel of all thought energy that exists within us. This is where we come from and return to. It is who we are, were and shall be.

By learning the path to it through many forms of relationship we will arrive at this point. Every type of relationship that we have had is part of this inner kernel of pure thought energy.

In the words of my Master, Ürgyen: 'To be a human being is the most blessed relationship of all, for you can know the state of suffering and of happiness and rise above both, to bring wisdom and beauty to those who are in despair and confusion. All of us can do this if we care. All we have is each other, we as the human race. It is our bond, common yet profound. It is our redeeming grace.'

6

THE POWER OF LOVE

Love is the most powerful force in the world. We are all born connected to love and whether we embrace it or ignore it, it is guiding us through our journey. The West has become consumed with the notion of romantic love. Much of the popular culture of Western countries is built around the idea of such love, the power it has, the longing for it and the loss of it.

The Bön beliefs about love are different. Although romantic love exists in the Bön culture, and is important, it is hidden quietly away and is not the focus of society. In the Bön view there are many types of love, all valid and important, and romantic love takes its place alongside other kinds of love, including the love between friends, between parent and child and spiritual love. In the Bön belief system the love that exists between people is only one kind of love, because love exists within us and in nature regardless of whether we experience personal and intimate love in our lives or not.

In the West the search for romantic love can become desperate and distract us from our own identity. Yet it is not always possible to find and keep such love. Sometimes the thought energies within us can only receive a certain amount of love before becoming dormant, for some of us have the facility to receive and give love more than others. This is not a good or bad thing, it is merely how our thought energies are constructed due to our time in the womb and the life we have led.

Romantic love is a fusion of the thought energies between two people that focus upon the awakening of desire and passion. The West is fuelled by romantic love and this has come about because the West is desperate to seek meaning, belonging and identity. Popular Western culture believes that this happens through the power of romantic love.

This is partly true. Romantic love is a catalyst for change, whether this is destructive or constructive. But although romantic love comes from desire, desires do not last long under its intensity, therefore it is skilful to regard romantic love as a lightning bolt which has come to wake us up and show us our potential for all types of love and loving. We have within us the potential for great love and this need not be of a romantic nature. We can love ourselves, our friends and families and those in the world whom we have never met.

In the Bön view the search for meaning, belonging and identity is not intertwined with romantic love, but is connected to the path of spiritual development which each of us chooses. Love, in all its forms, is vital to this path, beginning with love towards the self.

This great thought energy, which is so crucial to the development, evolution and continuation of the human species, is a universal thought energy understood in all dimensions and by all forms of living creatures. Love thought energy teaches us that we can overcome all things, that we are good, that we can move beyond our mistakes and that all our hurts and suffering can lead to a deep inner happiness.

In this chapter I will explain the nature of self-love and of falling in love and the difference between real love and passing desire. I will also explain the Bön beliefs about how to keep love with a partner thriving and strong, and how to resolve conflicts. I will outline the Bön view of appropriate sexual behaviour and the channelling of sexual energy and I will look at family relationships with parents, children and siblings.

LOVING YOURSELF

Loving yourself is important, whether or not you are in a love relationship with someone else. Loving yourself is not selfish, rather it is not loving yourself that is selfish. Self-love is necessary for a balanced and positive life and is crucial if you wish to undertake spiritual exploration. It is a courageous declaration of the value and meaning of your life.

Picture a world where everyone experiences self-love. There would be much less suffering, crime, poverty, cruelty and war. People who love themselves and feel good about themselves are far less likely to want to hurt others. There would be greater happiness for all.

Guilt, anxiety, fear and the countless whisperings of the everyday mind's disapproval and self-judgement, all undermine our ability to love ourselves. This vast obstruction, which takes place daily, is often hidden from our own awareness. We accept the thoughts of our everyday mind as all there is and don't see that beyond these critical, negative thoughts each of us has an unlimited capacity for love, towards ourselves and others.

Yet if we live without loving ourselves, we lose energy and vitality and the personality shrinks, so that we lose our individuality. We can end up becoming mean towards ourselves and others.

How do you experience self-love? It is simpler than you think, for no matter how tough and unloving you have been towards yourself, you have a deeper consciousness that continually experiences self-love. All you need to do is to bring this into your upper consciousness. When you do this, you will discover that it is your birthright and the spark of your humanity. Loving yourself is the starting point and the very foundation of all human existence.

To begin to release self-love, follow these guidelines:

- Change the nature of your thought energies, increasing skilful thoughts through meditation and reflection.
- Cut down on your responsibilities and obligations if these occupy a large part of your life. Too much busyness is simply a way of avoiding intimacy with yourself.
- Give yourself more calm and ease by doing things that make you feel good.
- Examine previous actions in your life that have, in your view, held you back.
- Take up a more integrated approach to your health through exercise, food and behaviour.
- Pray for blessings for the world and yourself.
- Make peace with people you find troublesome.
- Create quiet time to reflect and be grateful for what you have.

The advantages of self-loving are astonishing. You become contented, fulfilled, original, powerful and humble and you are able to listen to other people and really hear who they are. Self-love creates free will and delight. The inner light of self-love will sustain you even during times of darkness, despair and isolation.

The illumination of self-love is healing and, once discovered, will not let you down. Here are five practical ways to experience self-love:

1. Create your own safe haven, including your most

precious and important things in it. Sit and be silent, allowing yourself, in total stillness, to experience the thought energies of self-love.

2. Gently invoke the divine love within you to show how you could love yourself more in the everyday world. Allow this loving inner voice to speak to you until you are guided by it daily.

3. Share your discoveries about self-love with, in this order, a stranger, a friend, your partner, and then your family. This creates courage and understanding of your experiences.

4. Practise self-love in the small things of your daily life, through little acts of kindness to yourself and it will naturally flow into the bigger things.

5. Share what you have learned and encourage your children, friends, partner, family, colleagues, and even enemies to do this in their daily lives.

In time the thought energy of self-love will be with you constantly and will unfold as loving-kindness, towards yourself and everyone else in your life.

Sandy was a doctor who came top in her class at medical school and went on to specialise in paediatric medicine. She loved her job and cheerfully put up with the long hours she had to work, on top of the long journey she made to the hospital from her home each day.

When Sandy came to see me she looked worn out. She had a problem with her back which her colleagues had been unable to help, but it was easy to see that her back was more than simply the obvious symptom – her problems ran far deeper.

When I encouraged her to talk about herself Sandy painted a picture of a young woman who was incredibly disciplined and tough on herself. She never let herself have time off work, for sickness or anything else. On top of her job she spent time looking after her parents and sorting out her apartment. Sandy organised her life with lists of jobs to do and never found time to indulge herself or relax. She'd even given up playing squash and swimming, both sports she loved.

I suggested to Sandy that she wasn't very loving towards herself and she looked shocked. Once the idea sank in, she agreed that she constantly gave herself a hard time. No matter how much she did, she told herself it wasn't enough. I asked Sandy to go home and, over the next two weeks, follow the guidelines for releasing self-love. After that I asked her to include the practical methods of experiencing self-love for a further three months.

When Sandy reported back she told me that once she started being kind to herself she was amazed by just how cruelly she'd treated herself in the past. She began to enjoy being loving towards herself so much that she made all kinds of changes in her life. She moved nearer to work, paid someone to clean her apartment, made time for the sports she loved and cut back her working hours. The result? Six months after our first meeting a vibrant, joyful Sandy arrived to tell me that her back was just fine.

FALLING IN LOVE

When we fall in love it is because similar skilful thought energies in two people celebrate the discovery of each other. Thought recognising thought, as they meet. And as thought energy recognises its own nature it then shares itself with the two who hold it, in the form of love.

It is this mutual recognition of thought energy that causes the fires of passion, the dreamy states, the sweaty palms and the expectancy. When people feel that they have a meeting of souls it is because thought energies merge with each other. This can be for a lifetime, thirty seconds or one night. What determines the length of the connection? The lifespan of the thought energy each partner holds. When people fall in love, only to discover that they don't have a lot in common, it is because the thought energy has moved on.

The clue to how long a love relationship will last is there at the beginning, for the way it starts is the way it ends. A sudden and explosive start will lead to an explosive end: The faster two people rush into a relationship, the faster they will rush out of it again. Why? Because when you rush in, the thought energy is likely to burn itself out fast, or even to explode. When this happens damage is caused and people get hurt. People often travel at high speed when they are needy and wanting an intimate love relationship. They long for love and fall in love very quickly, but they are consumed by their own need and don't consider the other person. Such relationships can't last.

The more slowly and surely you go, the more likely it is that it will last. Thought energy needs to slow down and find order if it is to become stronger and last. When you go slowly the thought energy of love can build on itself, creating more and more loving thought energy.

It is possible to make someone fall in love with you by the power of thought energy, but it is not advisable, as this creates an artificial situation and is unskilful. It will always end in tears and is energetically damaging for both parties.

When Daniel met Rose he fell head over heels in love and

was convinced that she was his great love. He rushed her into a whirlwind romance and they became engaged after only three weeks. But within weeks Daniel started to feel conflicting emotions. He thought he loved Rose, but he wasn't sure.

He came to see me and I recommended that he do the Inner Friend Exercise from Chapter 5. After doing this exercise for several days Daniel began to see that he had created all kinds of fantasies for himself and projected them on to Rose. His romance had been what I term a 'love collision', a high-speed emotional accident, caused by dangerous driving.

Daniel had to come to terms with the fact that he had confused love with need. The deep neediness he felt inside was comforted by the idea that Rose was his perfect love. But Daniel knew that another person can never resolve such neediness, it must be done from within.

The next painful step he had to take was to explain to Rose what he had learned about himself and to break off the engagement.

Rose was deeply hurt and at first refused to have anything to do with him. But later they became friends, and Rose told him that she was glad he had discovered the truth about his feelings before they married.

The Nature of Lust

Like love, lust is thought energy, but in this case it is one generated by the unskilful thoughts of the everyday mind at a time when your body seeks to be charged up with energy.

When your energy gets really low you get lustful. The thing about lust thought energy is that you need to be careful where it takes you, for it can lead you into danger. Of course lust often arrives alongside love, and that is fine. But lust on its own is nothing but a cheap imitation of love. It is the spark of the lit match and if left to itself will simply burn out.

If you are worried by lust, especially if you feel it for someone else who is not your lover, send the thought energy of love to it. Quickly it will fade, automatically transforming itself into more positive thought energy.

If you feel lust towards your partner which is causing damage by getting in the way of deeper feelings, then direct your lust with your mind into your heart when it will become purified by the desire for balance and harmony.

How do you know, when you are drawn to someone across a crowded room, whether this is lust or real love? Check your body's responses. If it is lust you will feel purely sexual. If it is love you will feel a slower, more encompassing energy. If you allow yourself to be driven by lust into a series of brief flings which leave you feeling empty, then your thought energy is powered by loneliness, confusion about the real nature of intimacy and a search for innocence. People who go from one brief relationship to another want to be pure of heart and don't know how to achieve this.

Purity is not the same as vulnerability; true purity is knowing how to act at all times with the best intentions for yourself and others. To find such purity first stop the damaging behaviour which takes you from one relationship to another. Begin to look at the way you relate to the world, look inwards and make contact with the innocence and wisdom that are inside you. Use the Inner Friend Exercise from the last chapter to do this and to be at peace with yourself.

In this way you will be focusing on the healing thought energies of your body. Feel the sacred energy of your body and allow this to be the energy that drives your behaviour and choices.

The Appearance of Love

If someone is pretending to love you then they are using you as a practice tool in order to learn how to love themselves. They may not know this. It is quite possible for people to convince themselves that they are in love, when in truth they are not, they simply like the idea of being in love.

However, although they may not know the difference, you certainly will. This is a use of unskilful power and causes pain, suffering and anger. Trust your instincts: if you feel that you are not truly loved, if the signs of love are not right and if you constantly feel that something is missing, then you may have the appearance of love, but not the real thing. Love is not meant to be a source of pain, humiliation, grief, anger, emptiness or loss.

If this is your situation then it is better to remove yourself from it. Hard though this may be, it is a courageous step to take, for only by ending a pretence of love can you allow real love to come to you.

Soul Mates

The concept of soul mates is one that is often used lightly in the West to mean someone to whom you feel attracted or connected. In the Bön belief system soul mates share a deep, pure and spiritual love which exists of its own accord, with no effort from either of the people involved. Such love is deeply powerful and is often so overwhelming that it frightens those who feel it and they run away from one another, so that the love is never fulfilled. For this reason it is often the stuff of great love stories, filled with passion and loss.

If you share this kind of love with another person then it will survive whether or not you are together. The thought energy of soul mate love is self-creating and does not necessarily rely upon two people being in one another's company. The love between two people can exist independently of them and will become active again when they meet. This kind of love is a life path for the two people concerned, and will survive even if it is interrupted for many years.

Everyone has a soul mate, and they are usually, though not always, drawn to one another in a romantic relationship. You will almost certainly meet your soul mate at some time during your life and you will certainly recognise them, but this person may not be the one you share your life with or even have a relationship with.

If this happens then don't feel regret, or that it didn't work out. Think only that it *did* work out in the way it was meant to, for both of you. There is no place for regret in the love process, unless you have set out to hurt or misuse someone. Unintentional hurt needs to be forgiven, by both people, because it is simply the way things are meant to be.

Longing for Love

The Bön belief is that when you are unable to find the love you wish for then your love thought energy is not attracting a response from the thought energy of other people. In this case your thought energy needs to be healed and made complete.

A simple way to heal such unfulfilled thought energy is to draw back all your thoughts of loneliness and longing for love to you. Let them flow into your heart and, as they do, see them dissolving. As they dissolve pure, innocent, healing love flows over you, revealing to you the inner beliefs you have about love relationships.

This simple exercise will bring you the self-knowledge that you need in order to move forward.

KEEPING LOVE ALIVE

A relationship must be tended and given fuel for growth. This fuel is the thought energy that you put into the relationship and it is important that you make sure that this fuel is of good quality.

Communication

Skilful communication is based upon skilful thinking. In order to have a positive loving relationship you need to be able to communicate in a way that makes you and your partner feel mutually supported and powerful. If you do not communicate in this way unclear and unskilful thought energy starts to eat away at the core of your relationship and the vitality of your mutual connection is weakened.

The best way to communicate skilfully in a relationship is to understand the nature of the other person's thought energy. In order to do this you need to pay attention to these aspects of the other person's behaviour:

Their speech patterns
Their body language
The way they form ideas
The habits they keep

These four aspects of your partner show you when and when not to be communicating with them about important issues. Speech patterns and body language are a conscious projection of one's state of mind and will indicate what your partner is thinking. To communicate well, wait for a time when your partner is at ease and is connected to love. If this does not happen, send love into the situation.

The Importance of Trust

Trust is a mutual recognition between two people of each other's potential for goodness and the quality of their integrity. This means that trust can be developed by paying attention to how your thought energy and that of your lover's is applied in areas of importance that relate to your lives together. Although we sometimes feel instinctively that we can trust a person, genuine trust needs to be earned over a long period of time. In the Bön view, when you trust someone you give them part of your spirit and you bring that person into the lives of your family and all who know you. So waiting until someone has earned your trust is important.

Perfect Timing

The time when you approach relationship issues with your partner is very important. When communications go wrong it is often because the timing was wrong.

According to the Bön tradition there are three time cycles in each twenty-four hours when particular relationship issues should be raised. These are based on the natural rise and fall of thought energy for relationships. If you wish to have a favourable outcome then learn to use these three cycles, and the neutral periods in between, with wisdom and insight.

- The first cycle is from 6 a.m. to 1 p.m.
- There is a neutral period from 1 p.m. to 2 p.m.
- The second cycle goes from 2 p.m. until 7 p.m.
- The second neutral period is from 7 p.m. until 8 p.m.

- The third time cycle goes from 8 p.m. until 5 a.m.
- The third neutral period is from 5 a.m. to 6 a.m.

The first cycle from 6 a.m. until 1 p.m. is good for dealing with issues or problems of importance in the relationship. It is a time for gathering forces, strength and insight. It is also a time for peace-making and for mutual support.

The second cycle from 2 p.m. until 7 p.m. is the time for considering thoughts and actions, for discussion about different options and for mutual reflection.

The third time cycle from 8 p.m. until 5 a.m. is the time for deciding a final course of action.

The first neutral period, from 1 p.m. to 2 p.m., is a time to let things be. Do not force anything to do with your love thought energy because it will be troublesome.

In the second neutral period from 7 p.m. to 8 p.m. you should do nothing but spend time with yourself.

The third neutral period, from 5 a.m. to 6 a.m., is a time of giving thanks for the love in your life.

These time cycles relate to the flow of thought energy in the world and in your deep unconscious mind. If you use them you will tune into each other's physical, emotional and spiritual cycles and a natural structure will develop in your relationship, improving the quality of your love and nurturing mutual respect.

Conflict

There is always going to be conflict in any relationship, it is part of the nature of being together and is healthy and natural. Conflict that is handled well can contribute to the strength and quality of your love.

Conflict handled in an unskilful way will, on the other

hand, cause all kinds of damage to a relationship. Unskilful handling of conflict involves becoming defensive and attacking, using violence, escalating and extending the conflict and intentionally causing the other person pain.

To handle conflict skilfully you need to use your love thought energy in a tactical and strategic way and cut through to the heart of the conflict in order to reach understanding and mutual recognition. To do this simply listen to the conflict. Not just to the words, but also to the thought energy behind them. If you put your feelings aside and really listen you will know what to say to transform the conflict and reach resolution.

After this you can send a love missile of loving thought energy into the heart of the person you are having a conflict with. When it hits its mark, you will feel it and your conflict will no longer have a sting.

Kate and Sam had been married for over fifteen years and the relationship, which had been wonderful in the early days, had started to go badly wrong. Kate and Sam had endless rows about their thirteen-year-old son, who was getting into a lot of trouble at school. They would often begin rows just before bedtime, and both of them would end up miserable, tense and unable to sleep.

Kate wanted them to take a gentle approach to their son's problems, while Sam felt a tougher approach was needed. Each of them found it hard to listen to the other and felt certain they were right.

Kate came to see me and told me she was worried that their marriage was in danger. She loved Sam, but she felt angry with him.

I asked Kate to put her own feelings to one side and simply listen to Sam, next time they began a row. I also asked her to sit quietly on her own and send a love missile into Sam's heart. Finally, I suggested that they discuss their son's problems in the morning, between 6 a.m. and 1 p.m., a far better time for such a discussion than bedtime.

A month later Kate reported to me that she had listened to Sam, though this had been hard to do, and she had realised that he really did have their son's best interests at heart. She understood that she and Sam both loved their son and felt frightened that he would get into worse trouble, or begin taking drugs.

After two weeks of sending love straight to Sam's heart Kate suggested a morning discussion of their son's problems. This worked much better; both of them were more tolerant and listened to the other. Kate told Sam she knew he loved their son, and this allowed him to soften in his approach. They both realised that their endless conflicts were affecting their son, even though he did not hear them row. They understood that the best thing they could do to help their son was to stop fighting, to give him a lot of love and to agree sensible rules for him, which they would enforce together.

Six months later their son was behaving much better and Kate and Sam felt they had reached a deeper connection with one another and strengthened their marriage.

ENDINGS

Relationships end when your thought energy no longer connects with that of your partner. When this happens it is not necessarily a bad thing, it can simply mean that the relationship has run its course. Not every relationship is meant to last a lifetime. It may be that you have shared and brought to each other all that was needed and the connection between you is no longer relevant. When a couple part the love they shared will split in half, its energetic content going with each person according to their need.

When there is pain, shock and bewilderment it is because we grieve for the separation of thought energy that was once intimately joined. If you focus upon this thought energy you will come to understand why the love has ended. Sometimes people who are together are leading separate lives inside their heads and need to part.

In Bön societies couples are encouraged to sit together and contact their inner wisdom so that they know how the relationship will end. The Bön people believe that we all know in our hearts how our relationships will end, even if this is at the death of one or both of us. Knowing the ending might seem frightening to a Western person. But in the Bön way of thinking it will help you to get the very best from the relationship and to love and cherish one another while you are meant to be together.

When it's Worth Trying Again

How do you know when it's time to end a relationship and when it's time to try again? Some couples part and get back together, or reach the brink of break-up, many times.

The crux of whether it's worth trying to work things out is to recognise the kind of thought energy you create for each other. Is it constructive, destructive, ambivalent, or just plain thoughtless? If the way you think towards one another is essentially constructive, if there is respect and love at the core of the relationship, then it's worth carrying on.

When it's Time to Let Go

Even when you know that a relationship has run its course

it can be painful and difficult letting go and moving on. If you are uncertain about what to do then think about the thought energies you feel are underlying your relationship and decide whether they are essentially constructive or destructive. If they are the latter, then it is time to let go.

The pain, hurt and blame involved in a break-up can sometimes overshadow everything we do and feel. Yet trying to hang on to a relationship that has ended, or should end, creates bad luck, ill health, and turbulent lives. To understand the pain and gain self-knowledge from this experience it is important to remember to hold in your mind the highest good wishes and best intentions for the person that you once loved. Find the strength in yourself to do this, even if your relationship was a bad one or ended on bad terms. In fact the more painful it was the more important it is to use these skilful thoughts, as you will quickly dissolve any negativity this way.

In order to let go you must be ready to stand on your own two feet, create the independence you seek and make your life anew. To do this you must let go of all blame as well as all guilt. It is time to take full responsibility for your own actions and thoughts.

As you do this, while focusing on good thoughts towards the other person, the thought energies that supported your love will be able to disentangle themselves, creating a blessing of good fortune for the other person while freeing you. It will heal your heart and mind and create opportunities for a more profound love in the future, because you will not be taking any baggage with you from this relationship.

In the end, love in all its forms is essentially the celebration of who you are and can be. In loving someone you wished him or her life, vitality and good intentions. In ending it is best to continue with this frame of mind and heart, so that you can move into your new life without obstructions.

Love is an invisible goodness that finds its own journey through our lives and the only essence of love that we keep and learn from is the love we are prepared to give up. In the love you have experienced you have come close to the absolute goodness and universal beauty that is in all humanity.

Annette never liked to admit defeat. She was afraid of failure and after seven years of trying to make her relationship work she was still refusing to give up, even though it was causing her a lot of unhappiness. Annette came to see me wanting to save her relationship. I asked her to look at the nature of the thought energy underlying the relationship and to decide whether it was constructive or not.

Two weeks later she told me she had realised that the relationship was essentially destructive. Her partner had been violent, cruel and selfish towards her and she had accepted this behaviour, believing that she deserved it and that it was up to her to make the relationship work. Her fear of failure was holding the relationship together. Annette felt frightened and sad about ending her relationship, but she knew that it was the right course to take.

I asked her to sit quietly and concentrate on dissolving the unskilful thought energies in the relationship in order to let it go. I also asked her to direct love towards herself and her partner and to think about the freedom and potential for happiness each of them would find when they moved on.

This was very hard for Annette to do, especially as her partner did not want to end the relationship. She didn't know whether she would be strong enough to leave him, but as she did the exercises she discovered her own strength and resources.

Three months later Annette was able to leave the relationship. She did it with dignity and confidence and was able to wish her partner well.

Two years on Annette is with a new and very different man. They have a loving and healthy relationship and are planning to get married.

Marrying Again

People often marry, or live in a marital relationship, more than once in the search for happiness and belonging. This is part of each individual's path to self-knowledge.

The number of marriages you have is less important than the thought energies created within and without each marriage. The person who marries many times must be careful not to transfer the problems of one marriage to another and must, of course, consider the effects on any children of the marriages. People who marry many times often fall into the habit of multiple marriages because they have not learned the skills of finding the many qualities they need within one person and of resolving relationship issues.

SEXUAL LOVE

Sexual energy has existed as a profound thought energy in all forms of matter since the universes first began. This thought energy encourages growth, birth, life and death; it is the fuel on which all aspects of material energy operate. Your sexuality, whether you are gay, straight or bisexual, is a channel for your consciousness to express itself.

Sexuality is thought energy which seeks a way to express itself and to find its place in the material world. Sexual energy can be transformed and refined by the way you think about it, for it responds to thought energy and wise use of this energy can lead to greater spiritual and intellectual awakening. By tuning in to your sexual energy and the way you use it you will discover how you really feel about yourself. Sexuality and sexual energy are sacred and holy and if you abuse or misuse them, you abuse yourself.

Sex is a powerful thought force. Every time one person has sex with another person they transfer some of themselves to one another and absorb it into themselves. This can happen skilfully or unskilfully, depending on the way you see yourself and other people. Every time you take part in a sexual act your thought energies are absorbed by the other person, so if you do this without awareness you can weaken yourself. You absorb a little of everything from your sexual partner: thoughts, emotions, fears, hopes, desires, secrets, truths and their fate.

Sexual energy must always be treated with great respect, for it is pure and innocent and contains information that can guide us to higher states of consciousness. There are special paths to achieve this, including the path of celibacy, but for most of us who live in the everyday world the best path is one on which we strive to be as good and as responsible to ourselves as we can. This then helps us to discover our inner moral code, unique to us but universal for all.

The Power of Sexual Energy

Your sexual energy is a sacred expression of thought energy that seeks release, expression, knowledge, happiness and fruition. The power of sexual energy sits at the foundations of humankind, prompting our instincts and desires to come alive and express our humanity. This can be done skilfully or unskilfully. The power of sexual energy is immense and channels itself through our thoughts. If its power simply flows through us, directing us as it will, then we gain nothing from the process, but if by the skilful use of our thoughts we can slow it down and absorb it, we can then begin to understand it and transform it. We can choose not to be controlled by it. This is sexual liberation in the truest sense. Sexual liberation does not come from having large amounts of sex or from feeling sexually uninhibited. It comes when we know the dimensions and depths of our sexual energy and when we understand that we can choose to use it for purposes other than sexual activity.

Awakening Sexual Energy

Sexual energy is so powerful that it seeks expression in all human activities. It is skilful to learn to awaken sexual energy through all kinds of activities, not simply those that are obviously sexual. Any activity that you love and engage in fully will awaken your sexual energy. Try to sense it when you are doing something that requires all your concentration. When you feel energised, focused, have clear objectives and achieve a lot, then sexual energy is present.

To gain the benefits of this life-giving energy, sit quietly before you start a specific undertaking and direct sexual energy into it with your mind. It will bring clarity, success and creativity.

Sexual energy in itself is already pure and refined. It is the thought energies that we attach to it which can cause unskilful and unhappy outcomes. If you wish to refine and purify your sexual impulse, consider what thoughts and emotions appear within you when you experience sexual energy. Whatever you feel or experience, try to direct a steady stream of compassion and warmth towards these feelings. This will harmonise any grey or worrying areas that you are concerned about.

Choosing Sexual Partners

Sexual energy is sacred, and should be treated as such. So be careful who you have sex with. When you choose sexual partners you define the nature, quality and outcome of your sexual experience. The wrong person can cause your inner thought energies to be unbalanced and negative. Needy people can remove some of your vitality. It is better to know someone well before you have sex with them, so that you know whose energy you are taking on.

Wanting to have sex with someone is not enough, you must try to see beyond the moment and know why you want to have sex with them. Let your body and mind come together, rather than separating. You must have full understanding of your actions.

In the traditional Bön view you should not rush into sexual activity with someone you are simply attracted to. Wait at least one lunar month from the time you meet someone. If the attraction is real, the passion will build and the sexual exchanges, when you have them, will guide you both to a new type of happiness.

Your Moral Code

Unskilful sexual relations cause unhappiness and confusion. In order to tell whether a sexual contact with someone else is skilful or not you must first know what your individual ethics about sexuality and sex are. Many people have not developed their personal ethical framework, not because they are immoral, but simply because they have not considered this before. If this is true for you then set yourself some ground rules.

In the Bön tradition I come from the following points are normally raised to help an individual develop their inner integrity and personal moral code. They are:

- Sexual activity is a very intimate thing. If you have sex with someone you absorb part of their personality. Before having sex with anyone you need to be sure that you are ready for this responsibility.
- Do you trust this person with your vulnerable physical state when naked or in the rush of passion?
- Why do you choose to have sexual relations with someone?
- Does anger, lust, or greed motivate your sexual desires?
- Are you prepared to take responsibility for any unskilful outcome of your sexual actions?
- Do you regard sex and sexual energy as precious or as cheap and ordinary?
- Sex can take away your vitality if you become controlled by it.
- Are you prepared to let your sexual experiences give you wisdom?

Reflecting on these important points will help you to decide what your personal moral code is. Once you know, it is important to live by it in order to maintain your self-respect and integrity.

Promiscuity

Promiscuity, that is, having many sexual partners in a short space of time, actually destroys the free and natural flow of sexual energy through your body, mind and life. Instead it imprisons sexual energy through this pattern of habitual sexual behaviour.

Promiscuity comes from fear, rather than from the enjoyment of sexual interaction. To break free of this pattern you need to understand how precious and valuable your sexual energy is, and that you are destroying this great resource. Look deep within yourself for the fear that underlies your pattern of sexual behaviour. Is it the fear of abandonment, of not being loved, of being alone? This fear will only be increased through promiscuous behaviour. Changing your behaviour and becoming aware of your pure and valuable sexual energy will begin to dissolve this fear.

Many people feel guilt in connection with sex. The guilt you may feel about having sexual feelings, or having sex, will stop you from truly appreciating your sexual integrity and what you can offer to someone special. A safe and simple way to release the guilt around sex is to have a non-sexual massage once a week so that you start to feel comfortable with the idea of your physical presence.

Laurence was addicted to seduction. He thought he was a super-stud and moved from one woman to another, often finding a new girlfriend every two weeks and regularly having one-night stands. His good looks and charm meant many women fell for him and he thought his success with women and his non-stop sex life meant he was a real man.

Then, after twenty years of this, a young girl told him that he was a 'dirty old creep'. Laurence was shocked and began to think about his behaviour. He was in his late thirties and most of his friends were married with children. He had always laughed at them and considered himself luckier than they were. But now Laurence realised that he was lonely and his lifestyle was shallow and destructive.

He came to me because he wanted to change, but he did not know how. I suggested he do the Inner Friend Exercise and as he talked with his Inner Friend he discovered that, despite the hundreds of women he had seduced, he knew nothing about women or about real love. His fear of being unlovable had driven him from one woman to another.

I suggested that Laurence take time to think about his own moral code and what he wanted from a relationship. As he did this he realised that his behaviour had made him feel worse, not better about himself.

Laurence decided to do things very differently. He stopped seducing women and was celibate for a year. During this time he began to get to know women as friends, to talk to them about themselves and to think about what he really wanted.

He realised that he wanted marriage and children, he had just been afraid that no woman would truly want him. After his year without seduction he felt very differently about himself and his fear of being alone had begun to dissolve. A few months later Jill, a woman Laurence had become friends with, told him she loved him. Laurence realised that he loved her too and they began a very loving and happy relationship. Five years on they are married with two small children.

Rekindling Desire

When the desire for sex dies it could well mean your sexual energy needs to be repaired or is resting. Sexual energy moves in cycles in both the body and the mind and will respond to directions from unexpressed thoughts. The best way to heal this is not to be judgemental, guilty or angry but to consider why this thought energy has faded. Are there other areas of your life that are taking all your energy? It may well be that it simply needs time, patience and understanding. Don't push yourself or try to force desire. Trust that it will return when it is ready and when the circumstances are right.

If there is love between you and your partner and you both want to have a sexual relationship after a time of abstinence, then each of you will need to redevelop your awareness of sexual energy, in each other and in yourself. You can do this very simply and safely by spending time with each other, face to face, so close that you are almost kissing. Feel each other's breath. Slowly each of you blows gently into the other's mouth, one at a time. Let the energy in your minds and bodies join. Do this, as many times as you wish, until you feel ready to resume your sexual relationship.

LOVE IN MARRIAGE

The Role of a Husband

To be a husband is to behave as a guest in the house of your wife and never to be ungrateful or disrespectful. To be a husband is to assist in the growth of your wife's consciousness and happiness and to help cultivate the great feminine energy that can blossom in your relationship. As a husband you must give thanks for the celebration of feminine wisdom and abundance as you learn to experience the ancestral feminine wisdom of your wife.

This is the thought energy of what, according to the Tibetan Bön tradition, a husband should aim to be. It takes courage, for it is a meditation in human integrity and care. A man who can be a husband in this manner is a powerful man, strong in body and with a highly disciplined mind.

The Role of a Wife

To be a wife, according to the Tibetan Bön tradition, is to be the spiritual heart of the family, to know the minds of your children and husband and to control the wealth of your family. The thought energy of being a wife comes from the ancestral maternal line and accumulates in you as wife when you are in the womb. This does not mean that you are destined to be a wife, but only that you know what it is to be one. A wife is a healer and a powerful influence in the community, a symbol of the order of nature.

Balance in Marriage

In the nature of married life, relationships are always shifting, balancing and rebalancing themselves. Sometimes, though, the balance of power swings too much one way, or perhaps your lives become so busy that it is difficult to find time to spend together. It may also happen that you choose to reverse roles, that the husband has taken on the role of looking after the kids, doing all the household tasks and maintaining the home while the wife is earning the money to support the family. In such situations skilful thinking is needed to maintain the balance and harmony of the marriage. The following thought energy exercise will help you solve any issues that arise in your marriage.

Balance in Marriage Thought Exercise

You can do this exercise together or separately, but if you do it alone do it only for yourself and not for your husband or wife.

Sit quietly. Close your eyes. See yourself, your partner, your home, your children and everything that is a part of your family unit pulsing with a luminous green light. As you concentrate on this, begin to see the light cleaning and balancing your family and home. As it does this it extracts all the problems, blockages and concerns and with a flash transforms itself into a blazing white and yellow haze of light.

When this happens you will be filled with solutions and answers to your concerns. Pay attention to them and, after the exercise, follow as accurately as you can these inner instructions.

FAMILIES

Children

In the Bön tradition, as in many others, children are a great spiritual blessing upon the planet, the highlight of human evolution. We can learn a lot about the future, the past and the present from children.

The thought energy of children is directed towards exploration, the expression of innocence, the attainment of wisdom and the development of willpower. Childhood gives us the opportunity to learn how to develop our potential and children teach us the nature of divinity in the everyday world and remind us of the innocence that dwells constantly within our hearts.

Children are messengers from our own wisdom. When they thwart our sense of control, we may regard them as a nuisance, but in fact it is we who become distracted by the emotions and thoughts that children activate within us. Children are simply themselves, and direct and loving guidance enables children to continue to be themselves.

Understanding Children Thought Exercise

This is a simple exercise to help you understand your children more.

Close your eyes. Breathe normally. In your mind, see your child, or a child you know. Focus upon the energy of the child. Ask this child to be your guide to the domains of your inner consciousness. Be respectful and patient. Be quiet and contemplative. Then sit back and allow this process to begin.

If you have children of your own and there is a problem concerning your child focus upon their energy during this exercise.

Parenting your Children

The role of a parent is to guide a child to a state of emotional, physical and spiritual independence, and good parenting is the skilful expression of thought energy.

It is important for parents to understand that, as I explained in Chapter 2, according to the Tibetan Bön view children are already one year old at the time of their birth, with fully developed faculties of their own as well as those inherited from their parents. They inherit all their emotions and health from their fathers and their intellect, intuition and spirituality from their mothers.

Children are born having had their own life experiences in the womb, because thought energy is very powerful on the young human life as it develops inside the mother. In the following twenty-one years children act out these experiences and try to make sense of them.

To be good parents we must understand what our thoughts

are about helping to bring another life into the world and realise that our thought energies will stay with our children all their lives and be passed on to their descendants. Our thoughts can either uplift and enlighten our children or pollute them with our own shortcomings. If we can help them to love and to be tolerant then we have achieved a miracle.

Your own Parents

Your body and some of your habits have come from your parents. If your childhood was hard or you have many problems it's easy to be angry with your parents and to blame them for their ignorance and shortcomings. Yet we all have ignorance and shortcomings.

In the Bön view it is important to find a place in your heart to forgive your parents, no matter what they did, because until you forgive them you can't move forward in your own life. Forgiveness means understanding that the way they raised you was the only way they knew how to.

It is easy to be controlled by the hurt that your parents may have inflicted upon you, because these thought energies can be overwhelmingly powerful. But you can move beyond these experiences as you start to understand your own thought energies. You will see that the emotional pain you have experienced has been created because a part of you identified with and believed in your parents' unskilful thinking. But you do not have to keep hold of this legacy. Using skilful thinking you can choose to let it go, to forgive and to follow your own path.

Forgiving your Parents Thought Exercise

Close your eyes. Sit straight up so that your neck and spine are supported. Let your arms rest in your lap. See in your mind both your parents, or the most dominant or influential parent. Now see them slowly disintegrate, piece by piece, organ by organ, bone by bone until all that is left is a small pile of fine ash. Repeat this five times. Each time you do it, more of the negativity your parents gave you will be stripped away. When you have finished, bless your parents. Direct towards them pure love. Then forgive them without wishing for anything in return.

Brothers and Sisters

Ancient Bön teachings state that your brothers and sisters are expressions of the same thought energy that attracted you to this rebirth. You and your siblings are here this lifetime to share a similar lesson, to experience a common bond and to overcome the same obstacles, each in your own life journey.

You have brothers and sisters because you are all on a similar path of discovery about who you are and can be, even if on the surface you appear to have nothing in common. Each brother or sister you have will either express your own shortcomings or amplify your positive qualities.

When people don't like their siblings it is because they are rejecting the mirror image of their own shortcomings which they see reflected in their brother or sister.

Siblings are on earth to teach you to be compassionate and wise. We can learn from our siblings, and with the use of skilful thought we can see the common journey we share with them.

When you have adopted siblings, step-siblings or half-siblings they are gifts to your family line. They bring with them new opportunities for advancement, happiness, unity, love and success. Even if it is not apparent there is a deep thought energy connection between these siblings and you. Through understanding their story and recognising their needs you will discover why they are in your life.

Treat your siblings, like your parents, with love and forgiveness. The bond you have with them is meant to be and can't be broken by rejecting them.

THE WORLD NEEDS LOVE

Love is the one thing we are born with, we have throughout our lives and we take with us, to guide us on to the next part of our journey. Right now, wherever you are, there is love. Love in all its forms and guises is waiting to be discovered and expressed by your thought energies.

If you give love out to the world at large, it comes back to you many times over. The world needs love in order to continue; it regulates nature, the seasons and the evolution of humanity. When you have a spare moment send a thought of love out to bless the world at large. You can make a difference every day, by loving the planet we live on and everyone and everything on it. When you send out love other people respond by being kinder to their families, friends, neighbours, strangers and enemies. Love always finds a way to bring happiness, beauty and spiritual change.

7

TOTAL WELLBEING

A state of wellbeing exists when we have balance in our lives. In ancient Tibet individual balance was the focus and goal of most people, just as it is for us today. And then, just as today, to achieve this each person needed an understanding of the influences at work in their life and the ingredients needed to create a harmonious existence.

If the balance between the various essential elements of life is missing then stress, illness and unhappiness will result. Treating yourself badly, abusing your body in any way, doing work that you don't like, being in an unhappy relationship and eating unwisely can all have a powerful influence over your health. Maintaining good health is therefore a question of taking responsibility for your own welfare. Rather than becoming ill and then asking a doctor to cure you, it is better to prevent illness in the first place, or if you do become ill, to understand what you need in order to become well again.

In the West many people have no idea what truly good health and wellbeing feel like. Despite the high standard of living there are many influences that damage health. Over-processed foods, the culture of working long hours, the pressure to have many possessions, and pollution all act against good health. However, it is still entirely possible to maintain excellent health, a balanced life and a real sense of wellbeing, if this is what you choose.

No matter what your circumstances, you can do simple

and straightforward things for yourself to improve your emotional and mental health for ever. Prevention is not about strict, unbending rules which must be enforced no matter what. It simply means knowing yourself well, knowing your body's unique needs, what your mind needs and what kind of lifestyle will suit you.

Having fun, eating good food, sleeping well, exercising regularly, loving and feeling loved and doing work you enjoy are the key elements in a balanced life. But above all, to create true health you need to harness the power of skilful thought energy. Unskilful thoughts lead to ill health and lack of balance, while skilful thinking can be used to create the kind of life that supports your highest good and wellbeing.

THE THOUGHT ENERGY OF BALANCE

All the elements necessary for a balanced life, by their very nature, will shift from day to day. Life is full of ups and downs, good days and bad days, things that work out and things that don't. Even a job you love will have its negative side, the person you love will have off days and a good night's sleep won't always be possible.

Therefore in order to keep from being buffeted by the changing circumstances around you it is necessary to create a foundation which does not shift, and which is at the heart of everything in your life. This can be done with thought energy which, once established, will stay rooted with you, carrying you safely and calmly through whatever comes your way.

This Skilful Thought Energy is Veneration and Reverence for Life Itself

Balance that is lasting can only come from this veneration

and reverence. Life is sacred and beautiful. The things we do to live are not life, they are simply things we do because of the life we have. It is this life itself which we must value above all else.

Veneration creates a divine and intuitive connection with other people, animals, nature and the spirit of life. It is a two-way communication of the soul, a form of love which rejoices in the expression of the beauty of life and of its cycles, patterns, beginnings and endings. To venerate life is to acknowledge that you are in a state of perfect balance; it is a natural state within the heart of all people.

Reverence follows from veneration. When we venerate life we have reverence for it, for its wonders, its beauties and all that it gives us. Reverence teaches you to be content with the essential you which is unchanging and pure.

Veneration and reverence cannot be directed. They must simply be received through the natural grace that lies in our humanity. Allow yourself to receive them, in all that you do, say, think and feel. They are not hard to reach, because they are part of our human state. And once you receive them they will be at the foundation of your life, healing unhappiness and dissatisfaction and creating balance and wellbeing.

YOUR EMOTIONAL STATE

Many people are successful at what they do, but aren't happy doing it. The Bön practitioners believed that emotional thought energies can drive us to do things in our lives which, while successful and worthwhile on the surface, are wrong for us because they take us away from ourselves. It is not right to benefit others but not yourself; you need to do both.

Bön teaches that we all have an essential underlying emotional state, regardless of how we may appear, think, feel, or behave. The most important priority in creating a balanced life is to understand this emotional state.

Ask yourself this: Does your emotional state bring you happiness?

The ancient Tibetans knew that emotional thought energies affect what a person does for a living, the way they live, the way they treat themselves, how much they know and the quality of their lives. If your emotional state does not bring you happiness, or if you feel uncertain about what it is, then this thought exercise will help you to find clarity.

IDENTIFYING YOUR EMOTIONAL STATE

This thought exercise will allow you to identify and rebalance your underlying emotional state, the emotional thought energy that underpins your personality and your life. It will reveal the essence of what you feel and why you feel it. Do this exercise for as long as is necessary, at any time of day.

Sit quietly. Make sure you are comfortable and warm and that your eyes are gently closed. Now start to be aware of your breathing, and its rising and falling. Focus upon your physical heart and imagine, now, that you are breathing in and out of your physical heart. Now begin to feel, with every breath, an emotion rise and fall. This may be any emotion, simply let it come and observe it.

This emotion will be followed by another and another. As each emotion passes through your heart, your focused breathing extracts the essence of the emotion so that you feel it totally, throughout your body, then you let it dissolve into your heart until it has gone.

Let your emotions come and go until you reach an emotion that is not altered by your breath and does not dissolve. This is your essential emotional thought energy. As you identify it you will, at the same time, know what is needed to keep your life in balance.

This exercise will draw on your own natural wisdom. If your essential emotional thought energy is unhappy, angry or painful then you will understand what life decisions you have made based on this and what you will need to change in order to create balance and harmony in your life.

Your underlying emotional thought energy will change to a more happy and positive one as you begin to make changes in your life and to act from the heart of who you are and not from your emotional thought energy.

ILLNESS

Illness is the language of unskilful thought energies. When we're out of balance, living at the mercy of the endless random thoughts of the everyday mind, then we become stressed, run-down, exhausted and ill because illness will attach itself to any form of unskilful thinking. Your mind and body are one and the same, so when your mind is overrun with unskilful thoughts, many of them picked up from other people around you, then you become overwhelmed and the result is ill health. Good health comes from good and skilful thought energies and these are easy to create and keep, once you know how.

By understanding how you create illness and suffering in your life you become wiser and stronger. Illness serves a valuable purpose: it lets you know when something is wrong in your life and gives you the opportunity to change it. The illness you have is the one you need and will lead you, if you listen to it, towards positive change and good health. When an illness stays with you, or recurs regularly, it is because you are not listening to the message it is bringing you.

Terminal Illness

Many people suffer terminal illnesses and these, like all other illnesses, carry a message. However, no one should feel regret or self-blame when they become terminally ill. It is not a mark of failure, and in fact many of the most enlightened and wise spiritual leaders also suffer terminal illnesses. We are complex beings and it is not always possible for us to prevent or heal illness.

Of course in some cases it is possible, using the power of skilful thought, to heal yourself from a terminal illness. However, this is rare, and the blessing of terminal illness is often to be found through learning how to die well, with peace and acceptance.

TIBETAN BöN MEDICINE

A Bön practitioner will help a patient to gain insight about the cause and nature of their illness. The diagnosis will involve twenty-nine questions, the answers to which will reveal the patient's emotional, psychological and spiritual nature. The physician will also examine the patient's eyes, tongue, face, ears, hands and fingernails, analyse their urine and take their pulses. At the end of this the physician will be able to determine which of the three humours has the greatest influence upon the patient.

The three humours, wind, bile and phlegm, govern every aspect of how the body and mind function, as well as the world around us and the community we inhabit. We all contain all three humours, but one will be dominant, and we may have a second sub-dominant one also. Every human endeavour, no matter what it is, is created by the dynamic flow of the three humours and their accumulated thought energies. Like three great rivers of thought energy moving through all humankind, they govern who we are, what we are and what we do. When we are ill it is because our humoural energy is out of balance.

In my first book, *The Tibetan Art of Living*, there is a full description of the three humours, of the five elements, which are born from them, and of how to identify and rebalance your dominant humour. Here I will give only a brief description of each humour.

Wind

Wind is all things to do with thoughts, impressions, intuition, perception and ideas.

WIND OUT OF BALANCE

If you experience mental vagueness, talk more than normal, have memory loss, feel nervous, get excited easily, can't concentrate and feel agitated, mishear what you are told or cannot seem to understand what you read or hear, then you have a wind imbalance. Wind is also out of balance if you get angry a lot, cannot express yourself, get sick quickly or suffer emotional turbulence.

Wind is the thought energy of childhood. If a child has continual ill health of any type from conception until twenty years old, the wind thought energy is weak or damaged.

WIND IN BALANCE

If you feel very calm, with a razor-sharp mind, if you are generally happy for no obvious reason or if you are experiencing periods of strong intuition or any type of expansion in consciousness, then wind is in balance.

Prayer, meditation, singing, sharing, learning how to communicate or improve yourself are all things that enhance wind.

Bile

Bile is everything that is sudden, impulsive, urgent, immediate, exciting and challenging.

BILE OUT OF BALANCE

If you feel angry, violent or out for revenge, if you are suffering from addiction, if you are rude, grumpy and disrespectful, betray people or try to control others then bile is out of balance. Being fired, going bankrupt and messy divorce are all associated with an unbalanced bile state. Indications that bile is out of balance include a very red or a yellow complexion, depression and poor sight.

Bile is the thought energy of adulthood, from twenty years old until sixty. If you experience regular illness in this period then your bile thought energy needs to be repaired.

BILE IN BALANCE

If you experience huge direct bursts of infectious enthusiasm, sexual drive and charisma, if you feel ambitious and full of energy, then the bile humour is in balance.

Getting fit, improving your diet, losing weight, supporting environmental causes or charities generally, as well as wanting to improve your status in life are bile thought energies.

Phlegm

Phlegm is all that holds, contains, nurtures, restricts and supports the status quo. It is reliability, old-fashioned values and resistance to change.

PHLEGM OUT OF BALANCE

If you are mean with money, food or hospitality, if you find it hard to express your feelings, thoughts or physical desires, if you feel stuck or trapped, in a rut, can't find a job or can't make headway with a project then phlegm is out of balance. Ulcers, irritable bowel syndrome, coeliac disease, gut pains, hernias, constipation or diarrhoea and joint problems are all phlegm problems.

Phlegm is the thought energy of old age, which runs from sixty until death. If in this period you have illness on a regular basis, your phlegm thought energy is out of balance.

PHLEGM IN BALANCE

If you are capable of trust, reliability, integrity and honesty, if you save your money, if you are a responsible citizen, caring for your neighbours, if you eat good food, have fun with your children, read stories, bake and enjoy harmonious family activities then phlegm is in balance.

Relaxing activities such as massage, walking or painting enhance phlegm.

Keeping the humours in balance is vital to good health and wellbeing. By learning how to think skillfully, we generate less negativity and illness around us and the humours, and thus our lives become well balanced. This does not mean that life is always easy, only that you then know how to deal more easily with the problems life pitches at you.

According to Bön, health itself is a flux of thought energy which is constantly changing from one moment to the next. Good health has its own frequency of thought energy, which differs from person to person. When thought energy falls below this frequency, then the first signs of illness are experienced. Poor health presents itself in many forms and is not noticeable at first. So it's important to be aware of the signs that all is not well with you, even if you do not yet feel ill. Be aware of your feelings, your energy levels, your vitality and the way you look.

How to Turn Illness into a Blessing

Whatever illness you suffer from can be turned from a problem into positive and life-enhancing energy using this exercise.

To understand illness which appears periodically do the exercise once a week for twenty minutes. If you are very sick, do it as many times a day you wish, for at least a month.

Sit comfortably, or lie down. Close your eyes. Following the rise and fall of your breathing, feel your body, feel your organs, blood, bone and skin. Concentrate on them and as you do this feel your illness, focus upon it and see it releasing the reason why it is with you. Now see your illness starting to pulse with a brilliant orange light; all of you is flooded in this light and your illness starts to change its form, becoming less and less and creating good, pure and loving energy. Your body is healing and you feel vitality starting to surge from your heart, spreading through your body and mind, bringing understanding, forgiveness and wisdom.

You can also use this exercise to understand why someone else is ill and how they may recover. Towards the end of your session, direct the orange light to them and it will return bringing you information. Do the exercise for this purpose once a week for fifteen minutes.

When Alana came to see me she was twenty-eight and a total wreck. She had been ill since childhood, but no one could find out what was wrong with her. The many doctors she had seen over the years had suspected problems with her auto-immune system, or with her hormones, or that she had lupus, chronic fatigue syndrome or even leukaemia. Yet none of these diagnoses was correct. Alana was permanently exhausted, unable to eat properly, and so debilitated that it was a struggle for her to walk.

It was clear after examining her that her wind humour was deeply out of balance. In Tibetan medicine it is not important what name the illness has, what matters is what symptoms a person displays and what the imbalances in the body are. It was also clear to me that Alana had no concept of being well; she had lost touch with her own capacity for good health and believed that she could never be well. She did, however, have a lot of determination to change things, and this was a great help. I treated her for her wind imbalance and I taught her the Thought Exercise for turning illness into a blessing, which she promised to do three times a day for the next few weeks.

When she next came to see me, a month later, Alana was clearly improving. She had been very ill for seven days after beginning the exercise, but after this she had begun to heal. Slowly she was beginning to eat, to put on weight and to feel more energy. The exercise had revealed to her that the reason for her illness was a fear of life. Her older sister had died when Alana was ten, and this had triggered off her fear and thus her own illness. Understanding this helped Alana to make the choice to live and to have good health.

Three months later Alana was a changed young woman. She almost bounced into my office and told me that she was feeling great. Her periods, which had stopped, had returned, she was up to a normal weight and her parents were thrilled by the change in her.

Two years on Alana works as a herbalist and healer, she has a boyfriend and leads a normal and very happy life.

TAKING CHARGE

Balancing your life and creating wellbeing means being willing to take charge of your own life and your health. For many people this means becoming more assertive about what is right for them and learning to say no more often. Saying no to something or someone else is saying yes to yourself. When you refuse an extra task, those extra hours of work, the extra burden someone tries to dump on you, then you agree to protect and care for yourself.

Taking charge also means trusting yourself to know what's best for you. This means listening to your body and what it is telling you. So often illness comes because we ignore the messages our bodies give us.

Sometimes it is vital to say no to the suggestions and good intentions of others. Accommodating these can mean damaging yourself, if they are not right for you. Taking charge, and learning when to say no are much easier when you learn to develop and trust your own thought energies concerning your health.

If you are ill, or have been ill, use this three-point self-exploration to develop your skilful health thought energies. Answering these questions will inform you about the way you feel, think and act towards yourself and will give you the insight necessary to know how to take charge of your own recovery and good health.

1. How did you become ill, and how did you feel when you knew that you were ill?
2. Do you use your illness to influence people?
3. Do you believe that you can be free of illness and healthy?

Margaret worked for years in a food processing factory and one afternoon she felt very unwell and had to sit down before she fainted. She was taken home and over the next few days she became worse. She had developed hepatitis. It was a very virulent form of the disease and she lost weight and became afraid that she would die. Eventually she was taken into hospital.

The medical staff were doing everything they could for her, but none of the medicines was working. A member of her family asked me to come to the hospital to see what I could do, so after obtaining permission from the medical staff, I went to see her.

We chatted for a while and I explained to Margaret that it was up to her to take charge of her own illness and to trust herself to know what she needed. I asked her to answer the three questions above, as honestly as she could, and to act on the answers.

A few days later Margaret's son rang me to say that she had discharged herself from the hospital. She had put herself on a diet of her own choosing and was resting at home and spending time each day in prayer.

Two weeks later Margaret was out of bed and feeling better. Her doctors were astonished at her recovery. When I saw her next she told me that she had discovered a great wisdom within herself and that once she had been able to trust it she knew exactly what she needed. Saying no to the doctors had been hard, but it meant saying yes to her own way of healing, and this, she had known instinctively, was right for her.

RELEASING BODILY THOUGHT ENERGY

Your body has its own storehouse of thought energy, waiting to be released. It lies dormant in your nervous system, brain, heart, liver and reproductive organs. Each of these organs creates a particular resonance with thought energy and can therefore produce its own thought energy, enabling it to function and to regulate its own health as well as the general health of your body, your mind and your life.

As you do the exercises in this section they will heal you, teach you and make good things happen in your life, bringing you greater self-knowledge and happiness.

Your Brain

Your brain is a phenomenal centre of energy. It influences your thoughts and emotions and controls your body, instructing it in how to deal with the complexities of daily life.

Yet your brain lives in the past. Your senses tell it what is going on, but the information they relay, though it may seem instant, actually reaches your brain a second or so later. Therefore, we always are living in the past, although we imagine it to be the present.

This is the Bön view of how we understand our reality as it is conditioned by our senses. To experience reality as it happens, we must go beyond the senses, and this skill can be achieved by amplifying the power of the brain.

Tuning Into Your Brain

This exercise will amplify your brain's powers and is also good for helping with anxiety, depression, learning difficulties, money problems and issues of sexual faithfulness.

For maximum benefit do the exercise for at least twenty minutes a day over a nine-day period, then rest for nine days and repeat the exercise for nine days. Within two days of beginning it you will be aware that your perceptions, insights and knowledge have increased.

Do this exercise six times a year and you will find that after two years your brain will be in an amplified state continuously. Children should only be taught this by a Bön expert.

Sit quietly, with no distractions. Close your eyes. Let your breathing be normal. Focus your attention between your eyebrows just at the top of the bridge of your nose and concentrate on this for a few minutes.

When you have done this, focus on the back of your head. You will feel a little lump and a cavity there, just above the top of your spine. Focus all your attention into this area for several minutes.

Now direct the front and back areas you have focused on to move into the centre of your head, within your brain. As they meet, see a globe of white light starting to shine inside your brain, gently at first then becoming brighter and brighter. Concentrate your attention on this light.

This light now starts to flow from your brain out through your body, finding its own way – you do not have to direct it – out into your senses, your sight, smell, touch, taste and hearing. If you have lost one of these senses this will make no difference, as energetically they still work.

Now see your five senses starting to glow with this white light. Every sense becomes heightened, taking in information that you are not normally aware of. At this point your senses start to expand, flowing through your body back into your brain and making a thought energy connection, so that each sense becomes a conduit, a source of vision for your brain.

Now direct the white light into your brain again, increasing its natural functions and abilities. You don't need to know or list these. Feel your brain start to become enhanced and to release functions and abilities that you were not aware of.

Mark had always been troubled by anxiety. It had become a pattern established in childhood and continued into his adult life. He had a good job and a loving girlfriend, but this did not help him and his anxiety was putting a great deal of strain on his relationship.

By the age of thirty-three Mark had problems sleeping, suffered from ill health and seldom enjoyed life. Medication had not helped him and his anxiety dominated his life to the point where he was unable to take part in many ordinary activities.

Having tried many approaches which had not worked Mark came to me for help. I taught him how to tune in to his brain and asked him to do the exercise for nine days and then to report back.

When he returned Mark told me that within a few days his anxiety had started to dissolve and that he felt calmer, more balanced and more focused in all his activities. After nine days he repeated the exercise and found that he was improving daily, to the point where he felt he could resume normal life.

Mark is now happily married and enjoying his life. He is healthy and sleeps well and his anxiety is a thing of the past. He uses the exercise regularly to keep his life in balance.

Connecting To Your Central Nervous System

Your central nervous system is a living expression of pure

thought energy. It is a master communicator and it contains profound knowledge within it about our physical reality and the origin and evolution of our species. When you connect to your nervous system you start to become aware of the connections between all things in nature. Releasing the thought energy of your central nervous system will have a profound impact on your life, bringing you clarity, insight and the ability to make changes. It is particularly helpful in treating illnesses of the central nervous system, anger, heavy workloads, the need for advancement in your career and problems connected with property disputes.

Do this exercise in the same way as the one for the brain; that is, for nine days, with a nine-day break and then another nine days of the exercise. Do it no more than six times a year.

Close your eyes. Be as quiet as you can. Place your focus at the top of your spine and then let it travel from the top if your spine down to its base and back up again. Let it take its own time. Do this three times.

When this is completed, move inside your spinal cord with your mind. At this point, your nervous system will respond, taking your mind on a journey through your body.

When you have finished this journey, let your focus come to rest at the very top of your spine, at the base of your head. Now send a soft blue-white light into your central nervous system. See the light expanding beyond your body to an area of ten feet around you, above you and below you. Rest in this expanded state.

Then start to feel all the information that flows to you. Receive it without trying to understand it all, it will explain itself to you. Trust this.

Listening to the Wisdom of your Heart

Your heart does more than just pump blood, it also influences your emotions and thoughts and is influenced by them. You can learn a lot about the real state of your physical and emotional health and the true nature of your vitality by listening to your wise heart.

This exercise is very relaxing and teaches you to connect with your body, so that you can understand it better. It is especially good for helping to heal heart diseases and conditions, a broken heart or problems connected with betrayal. It is also very helpful for reuniting families, finding a home and creating happiness and love.

Do this exercise for ten days, taking as long as you need. After this do it for no more than twenty minutes once a month. Do it for three months, then stop for three months, then do it for another three months.

Sit quietly. Close your eyes. Listen to your heartbeat. Let the sound of your heart beating be the sole focus of your attention. Let your mind now flow around your body with the blood pumped by your heart. When you return to your heart, place your mind into all its cavities. Leave your mind there, open your eyes and rest.

Loving your Liver

As your liver cleans your body, so it can clean your life of sludge, rubbish, unneeded emotions and pain. The liver is a detoxifier, for your body, your mind and your life. Doing this exercise will help to ease problems, bring you solutions and improve long-standing health issues. It is also good for treating liver disease, addictions, metabolic illnesses and impure behaviour and for sorting yourself out so that you can make a better life.

If you don't know exactly where your liver is, look in a book.

Do this exercise for twenty minutes, once a month, each month throughout the year.

Sit quietly without distractions. Focus your attention upon your liver and travel inside it. From within your liver feel how it cleans your body. From within it see a shining green light emerge from it. Let this light purify the liver, then allow the light to purify your body of illness, pain and fatigue. Allow it to purify your mind of negative behaviour, emotions and unskilful thoughts. While keeping your focus inside your liver, rest.

Josie felt her life was stuck. Her career as a singer was not going anywhere and the rest of her life felt in limbo too. She was in debt and felt under pressure from her family and friends to give up singing and find another job. Josie loved singing and was determined not to give it up, but she didn't know how to find the break she needed.

As she did the liver exercise Josie began to understand why her life was so stuck and to realise that she needed to change the things that were not working. She moved cities, changed her agent and developed another singing style. Within a year she had a recording contract and today she is a successful jazz singer.

Tuning in to Your Reproductive Wisdom

MEN

Male reproductive energy is part of the sexual energetic structure of male thought energy, but it is also far more than that. It is the aspect of reproductive thought energy which enables the world and nature to be made. Male reproductive thought energy brings awakening and understanding of why things are as they are.

This energy is to do with stimulation, direction and reaction. It erupts into action then subsides, it seeks to be acknowledged, it challenges, it asks questions and demands answers.

This exercise is excellent for conceiving children and for healing male sexuality issues, reproductive conditions and illnesses. It helps to create confidence in timid men and can heal long-term depression.

In urgent cases do the exercise for fifteen minutes once a day for two weeks. Otherwise do it once a month on alternate months.

Sitting quietly, place your mind into your groin. Focus upon it and allow your concentration to be restful and still. Start to sense the immense power of this energy. Allow the energy to move up into your body, finding rest in your heart. Feel the upward flow of the energy into your heart and, as you feel it, allow the energy to bring understanding, healing and vitality into your body.

Louis had problems in his intimate relationships with women. He found it hard to let any woman come close to him, he was not confident sexually and he had no sense of male pride. His self-esteem was very low and he found it hard to imagine why any woman would want him.

Then he met Sandra. She fell in love with him and longed to be close to him, but Louis kept pushing her away and was in danger of losing her altogether.

When we talked it was easy to see that Louis was missing his sense of maleness and manhood and his understanding of all the blessings of being male. He began the exercise for tuning in to his reproductive energy and within two weeks he felt many changes. He began to feel good about his body and to take pride in it and feel tender towards it. He found his sexual vitality increasing and he was able to allow Sandra to get closer to him emotionally, without feeling threatened.

WOMEN

Female reproductive energy knows the 'whys' and 'hows' of everything. It is profoundly powerful but extremely quiet; it moves in the very deepest dimension of life thought energy. Through this energy the answers to all kinds of questions can be discovered and all kinds of events can be made to happen, born from thought energy.

This exercise is especially helpful for all female reproductive illnesses, for developing female consciousness and spirituality and for awakening the wise woman within and shaking off all negative beliefs and behaviours.

Even if your womb has been removed physically, it is still present as thought energy.

Do the exercise for thirty minutes at a time, as often as you like.

Close your eyes, breathe normally and let mind fill your womb. Be there quietly. As you do, a gentle pink light starts to shine from within your womb and flows throughout your mind and body, and back, gathering itself in your womb. Keep your focus in your womb. This is all you need to do.

Patti longed for a baby. But she and her partner had tried to conceive for five years, with no success. Medical intervention had not helped and Patti feared that she would never be a mother. She watched her sisters and friends having children and felt that she was not a proper woman and had failed.

When I met her Patti was very unhappy and her relationship was under great strain. She began the female reproductive energy exercise and did it every day for a month.

During this time the way Patti felt about herself transformed. She felt more appreciative of her body and began once again to feel good about being a woman. Her relationship improved and two months later she conceived.

GOOD HEALTH

Many people live with less than good health for so much of the time that it's easy to forget what real, glowing, vital good health is like and how precious it is. There are as many ways to be healthy as there are people. However, there is only one truth behind all the different ways, and this is that the way you think creates your health.

Within your body, regardless of its state, appearance, age, or condition, good health and beauty exist right now as pure and powerful thought energies waiting for you to recognise and claim them. You are living with good health, day by day, night by night, in every moment of your life. You can unlock and claim this healthy thought energy very simply. It is waiting for you and needs only to be acknowledged. The power to heal does not come from outside you, but from within.

THE GOOD HEALTH THOUGHT EXERCISE

Use this exercise to reach the wonderful good health energy inside you.

Do this thought energy exercise once a week, or more often if you feel the need, giving yourself plenty of time. Allow it to take as long as it needs, don't rush it. The best time to do it, for maximum results, is in the early morning just before the sun rises. But doing it at other times will still be of great benefit.

Sit or lie down on your back. Make sure your head is straight and your body weight is evenly distributed. Close your eyes. Let your breathing be relaxed and as even as possible.

Now imagine your body, your emotions and your thoughts, from the centre of the top of your head, down throughout your body, to the tips of your toes, starting to dissolve slowly, piece by piece, into a small pile of fine red powder. All that left behind is you, your personality and consciousness. Stay like this for at least ten minutes if you can. During this time, see yourself clearly as you wish to be: vibrant and healthy.

When you have done this, choose something that is important in your life but which you know does not support your good health and which you will now give up. This could be an activity, a habit, an ambition, a relationship or an object. Now take a mental image of what you are to give up and cast it down upon the powder. As the image of what you are to give up hits the powder, the powder bursts into a column of flame, brilliantly blue, white and hot. Your consciousness enters into the centre of this pillar of fire.

Now see your body starting to grow as new around you, healthy and strong. You sense and feel every part of your new body and mind being forged into life, then your consciousness merges and becomes one with your body.

At this point, as the fire is still swirling around you, give thanks to whatever force or god you believe in. Ask to be blessed with this new creation. Breathe in, and allow the pillar of fire to flow within your body. Slowly open your eyes.

Joe had never really felt well. He was only forty, yet he seemed much older and always seemed to have several things wrong with him. His back would play up, or he'd have a bad knee, or his stomach would give him problems, or he'd develop a mild skin complaint. Joe worked long hours as a truck driver and couldn't afford to take time off work, so he put up with his complaints and got on with life.

It was Joe's wife, Maggie, who suggested he come and see me. When he arrived he told me he didn't know why he'd come and didn't expect me to help. He said there was nothing wrong that he couldn't deal with.

I asked Joe if he knew what it felt like to be really well. He looked surprised and admitted he didn't. I asked Joe to do the Good Health Thought Exercise every day for a month and then to let me know what happened. Rather grumpily he agreed.

A month later a smiling Joe arrived back to see me. He had done the exercise, very sceptically and without expecting anything to happen. As part of the exercise he had agreed to give up drinking coffee. He drank several very strong cups a day and knew it wasn't doing him a lot of good.

To his surprise Joe had begun to feel better within a week. After two weeks he noticed that his health complaints had improved and after a month he told me he had no complaints at all and felt in great shape. He had started going to a gym, cut down his working hours and started spending more time with his wife and children.

The exercise helped Joe to get in touch with his own inner good health, and the more this happened the more he sensed what he needed to make his life happier and more balanced.

THE FOOD YOU EAT

It would be impossible to create wellbeing without looking at the food you put into your body each day. Your food becomes a part of you, fuelling the wonder that is your body. In Tibetan medicine food and diet are very important. Whatever is put into the body will be absorbed and the body will do its best to make good use of it, however good or bad it is.

When you eat a food you are absorbing the energy of anyone and anything that has been in contact with the food, along the chain from its origin to your table. A food that is highly processed or has travelled halfway across the world to you will have picked up all kinds of energies as it travelled, and some of these may be harmful.

It follows then that the simpler the food chain and the purer the food, the better it will be for you. To eat seasonal, organic, locally grown foods is ideal.

Diets

Dieting just for the sake of losing weight is bad for your physical and mental health. Such diets tend not to work, and if they do work it will be at the expense of your health. Learning to trust your body to tell you when it has had enough is far better than any diet. Never eat until you are completely full; allow your stomach to fill half with food and a quarter with liquid at any meal.

Bön medicine suggests that, once every two years at the end of winter, you should spend around three weeks eating more grains, pulses and proteins than normal. This will improve your vitality and wellbeing.

It is also fine to follow a sensible detox diet of your choice, in order to cleanse and rest your digestive system. The best time to do this is for ten days at the very start of each season. This timing will allow you to reap the maximum benefit from the detox, increasing your health and prosperity.

How You Eat

In the Bön system the way you eat is even more important than what you eat. An organic meal, eaten hastily in front of the television, will be of less benefit than a burger and fries eaten slowly, peacefully and lovingly.

Here are the Bön guidelines for healthy eating:

1. Be respectful of your food and of the act of eating.

2. Never rush your eating.

3. Never eat while doing something else, such as reading or watching television.

4. Never eat when angry. Wait until your anger has passed.

5. Always give thanks for what you are eating and eat it with love.

To eat in haste, or in anger, will lead to weight gain, ill health, addictions to sugars and fats and anti-social attitudes.

Eat with love and respect, taking your time and appreciating what you are eating. This will lead to good health, wisdom, love and vitality.

Matthew was a fitness instructor, but in a 'down' period of his life he started to eat fast food. It comforted him and seemed to take away his stress and anxiety. Soon he was addicted to this kind of food. He loved milk shakes, hamburgers, and fried food generally and he couldn't stop eating it. By indulging in this comfort eating he piled on the pounds and after two years he was very overweight and no longer able to do his job. Matthew woke up one day feeling desperate.

He came to see me and as we explored his anxiety and the problems he'd had in his 'down' period, he discovered he had merely transferred his problems into his eating. I treated Matthew with herbs and acupuncture and asked him to begin exercising. I also encouraged him to start giving thanks each time he ate, to eat slowly with respect and love and to treat his food as sacred.

After two weeks Matthew came back to tell me that this approach to food had changed him for ever. Giving thanks and respect this way had made him realise that he was slowly poisoning his body and mind with fast food.

Within a month his expertise as a fitness instructor was back in action and he felt strong, healthy and good about himself. His craving for fast food had disappeared and he took pleasure in eating as well as he possibly could.

EXERCISE

Exercise is important in educating your mind and body about how to stay healthy. But it is only of any value if your mind, emotions and intellect are integrated with the physical action you take. Exercising your body without making this consciousness connection will be of some benefit, but this will be limited and will not create genuine good health. The skilful thought energy necessary for wellbeing must be involved.

These simple Bön exercises, called the Eight Steps, are based on the Bön Kum Nye exercise system and while exercising your body will also harness skilful thought energy. Many of my patients have gained great benefit from them. They will help to keep you trim, sharp, content, sensitive, full of common sense and compassionate. You can do them anywhere at any time.

THE EIGHT STEPS

Wear comfortable clothes. Stand upright with your feet slightly apart. Let your arms hang loosely at your sides.

---

1 Begin with your arms by your sides and then lift them slowly up until they are stretched out in front of you. As you lift them up think of a great weight pushing down upon them. Now, with your arms still outstretched, slowly lift your right hip, leg and foot, bending at the knee. Gently lift your knee as high as you can; when it is at waist level, or as near as you can reach, slowly extend your leg and foot out in front of you. Leave it there for as long as you can, then slowly bring it back to rest and do the same with your left hip, leg and foot. Now slowly bring both arms to rest at your sides. Rest in the standing position while breathing slowly and calmly. This prepares the body for the other seven exercises while increasing balance and improving stamina and circulation.

2 Breathe in through your nose, and imagine that you are swallowing your breath. Let it sink into your navel. Do this eight times. It creates physical and mental power.

3 Spread your legs as far apart as you comfortably can. Then place your hands on your head with the fingertips touching each other in the centre. At this point stretch out through your elbows while pressing your hands down on to your head. Stretch up through your spine, neck and head, so that the pressure from this stretch meets the pressure from your hands.

Stretch down through your legs from your hips to your feet. Do this for three minutes. Then stop, slowly bringing your arms down and your feet together.

4 Open your mouth while in the standing position and stretch your upper and lower jaws as much as you can for up to three minutes. This stretches the face muscles, the neck and the inner ear and increases youthfulness.

5 Stand with your feet and legs together, arms by your sides and then lift up on to the balls of your feet. Stand like this for as long as you can as it relaxes and vitalises your organs and detoxes the body.

6 Rub your body from head to toes with the palms of your hands, in long, strong, sweeping motions. Do this for at least five minutes. It improves the skin, breathing and mental clarity.

7 Sit down on the spot that you were standing on. Cover your eyes with your hands. Focus upon your eyes. See vitality flowing from your hands into your eyes, your brain and through your nervous system, bringing peace, balance and vitality.

8 Begin the next exercise by drinking two small glasses of still water, the purer the better. Drink slowly and as you do, see the water becoming full of sparkling incandescent balls of light. Feel this light travelling down through your gut and being absorbed into your mind and body. This leaves you clean, pure and at rest.

You can do these exercises at any time of the day, but you must always do them in sequence, to completion. If, however, you are stressed out, feel tired, are ill or have a headache or if you're travelling or have jet-lag, do any of the eight that you feel attracted to.

SLEEP

Most of us spend many hours of our lives in sleep. Because of this the ancient Tibetans developed highly sophisticated methods of healing illness, developing wisdom and gaining enlightenment while sleeping.

The time we spend sleeping is valuable and enriching and needs to be treated with respect. Pushing your body to function with too little sleep is like expecting your car to run on too little fuel. In the end it stops going.

The amount of sleep each person needs is an individual choice. Some people need more, others need less. Use your knowledge of yourself to work out how much sleep you need and then make sure that you get it.

THE SLEEP THOUGHT EXERCISE

Use this exercise to improve the quality of your sleep, banish insomnia and enrich your sleeping hours. It is a safe and effective method of healing and balancing your thought energies.

It is particularly useful if you suffer from mood swings, excess anger, or feel that your emotions always get the better of you. You can also use it if you feel that you are too sensitive or become easily swamped by other people's thoughts or by events in life or on the news. It will help any type of phobia, fear or anti-social behaviour.

Start about thirty minutes before you would normally go to bed. Make sure that you are warm and comfortable, with your head, neck, arms and back well supported. Make sure your spine and hips are relaxed and straight. Close your eyes. Start to focus on your normal breathing pattern. Allow it to slow down, lengthen, and deepen just a little bit. Now see, in your mind, a soft white pinprick of light, blinking like a far distant lighthouse. Think of yourself floating on the wind and moving slowly towards this light. Your body feels weightless. All that exists is you, your mind, and the soft blinking white light. At this point, you focus upon the mental state or behaviour that you wish to heal. Put it in front of you and the light. As you do this, see the light increase to an enormous size, still blinking. Its gentle rays will now start to dissolve the mental state or behaviour.

You now start to hear a beautiful bell-like tone coming from the light, and you experience an overwhelming sense of purity, peace and healing. As if it were the sound of the wind in trees or soft lapping waves, you hear all around you a voice saying, 'Sleep, now, sleep.' You fall asleep, to wake at your normal time.

Do this every night for at least three months. Do not worry about how long to do it for as the idea is that you fall asleep while doing it and it works while you are sleeping. Well before this you will feel gentle changes taking place both in your mind and in your behaviour.

Michael had suffered from many different types of phobias, behavioural problems, obsessive thoughts and insomnia since his early teenage years. When he came to see me, he was fifty and despite all his problems he had successfully held down a job as a shift worker at an international airport. But finally he felt that it was all getting too much for him. He was afraid he was going to crack up.

I gave him the Sleep Thought Exercise and asked him to focus on each of his problems in turn while doing it. He was not convinced, but agreed to try it. Within three weeks of beginning the exercise he was starting to sleep through the night and to wake with a true sense of peace, balance and contentment. After six months many of his conditions had completely disappeared and he was sleeping normally, his much longed-for eight hours a night.

At this stage Michael found the courage to consult a psychologist, who helped him to overcome his remaining psychological problems.

Michael had turned his life around and his wife was overjoyed to have a relaxed and happy husband, no longer in mental anguish.

THE HEALING POWER OF LOVE

Health, in whatever form it takes, is a strand of thought energy that comes from love. Love is the ultimate medicine and the most effective healing thought energy that exists.

The thought energy of love is humanity's greatest gift to itself, for love can recognise itself in all things, and in the worst and best of times love is always where we least expect to find it. From a war zone to the workplace, from the sick bed to the schoolroom, in raindrops, in the healing of a broken heart and in the last breath that we take, love is always with us.

I have seen many sick people turn from abject suffering to bright new lives when they experience the healing power of love. They may think that it comes from some external force, but in fact they have simply attracted the thought energy of love that exists, potent and accessible, within them.

How can we experience this love on a daily basis? How can we use it to be healed and to heal? Simply by sitting and being still. By discovering the importance of silence and listening to your inner self you will find the thought energy of love. You do not need to do any special meditation or to be qualified in any way, because it is in this one area that all people in the human race are equal. Everyone can experience love.

Take five minutes three times a day, fifteen minutes in total, as you wake, before you have lunch and before you go to bed.

Close your eyes and listen to all the sounds around you. Listen to all the sounds within your body and the chatter of your mind and regard all the sounds you hear as your friends.

Now listen through the sounds and you will experience the thought energy of love. It is endless, adaptable, wise and accessible, personal and universal, joyous and stern. It is childlike yet ancient, innocent yet knowing; it is all that you are and can be and shall be.

Leigh was in his mid-thirties and hugely successful, a self-made man who had been able to buy the different members of his family a house each. He was also married to a lovely wife with a lovely baby son, but all the potential joys of his life meant little to him because Leigh was in a spiritual crisis.

His health was gone, he felt permanently ill and his soul was in despair.

When I talked to Leigh it soon became clear that he was a very angry man and that his anger had been eating away at him for years.

I asked Leigh to listen to love, three times a day. He was impatient and didn't want to do it, but agreed in the hope that it would help him.

Three weeks later I saw Leigh again. He told me that as he had done the exercise he had found himself connecting with a powerful stream of love. As he did this, his anger began to dissolve and Leigh felt love filling his life. Most important of all, he discovered spiritual love, the spark that lies behind all things. He learned how to apply his new-

found spiritual love to every part of his life. His enterprises prospered and he shared his wealth with more people.

When his wife died suddenly Leigh suffered another deep crisis. But the love he had found carried him through his grief and gave him the strength to care for his son.

PERFECT BALANCE

Achieving perfect balance in your life doesn't mean sticking to a rigid plan or depriving yourself of things you enjoy. On the contrary, it means having plenty of what you enjoy.

Too often in the West I see people who believe that good health and balance mean hard work and discomfort. They get up at dawn to go to the gym, eat foods they don't really want to eat and follow a regime they can't keep up for more than a few weeks or months. Then they collapse and decide that keeping healthy was too demanding.

I ask them to start again, with a whole different mindset. Staying well means living a life you enjoy and which feels manageable and straightforward. It means having fun, laughing often, taking time out just to do nothing sometimes, exercising in a way that feels pleasant or enjoyable and eating with delight. There is no room for fanaticism, going for the burn or self-punishment in such a life. Just as the way you eat is more important than the food you are eating, so the way you live is more important than the individual ingredients of your life. Live the life you truly want, without being a slave to anyone else's rules. Work hard, but play too. Live with generosity towards yourself as well as others. Listen to what your body tells you and trust it to know what it needs. This is the basis of the skilful thinking which will give you consistent wellbeing.

8

THE JOY OF FREEDOM

People across the world and throughout the centuries have searched for freedom, fought for freedom, bargained for freedom and died for freedom. Freedom is both a practical, measurable quality, and an ideal state. It is both the right to do and say as we please and the ability to experience spiritual heights. In the West there are freedoms that are envied by others in the world, and at the same time an absence of freedom which keeps so many people in a state of longing.

Those in the West tend to see freedom in material terms. The amount of freedom people have is generally judged in terms of money, political rights, ownership of a home and choices about where to live, what work to do, what schools to send children to and what holidays to take. These things do matter. Democracy has been hard won and is precious. The right to vote, to speak out, to earn well and to make lifestyle choices are important.

However, in the West there are many people who have all these things and who still do not feel free. They feel trapped, weighed down with work, duties, responsibilities, pressures and stress. This is because they do not have inner freedom – the most important freedom of all.

In the ancient Bön view freedom exists as an independent state, outside the rights and liberties that all human beings are entitled to. This kind of freedom is created through skilful thought energy and the cultivation of this thought energy is vital to a true sense of inner freedom, which can exist no matter what your outer circumstances. External freedoms will always come and go, subject to changing circumstances and energies. But true inner freedom, once achieved, is a constant which will bring with it a sense of peace, harmony and understanding.

In this chapter I will begin by asking you to look at what freedom means to you, and what kind of freedom you wish to achieve. I will outline the fourteen types of freedom recognised by Bön and finally I will give you an exercise called Awakening the Five Protectors. This thought exercise is profound and is the key to awakening and discovering freedom in all its forms. Whether the freedom you are seeking is material or spiritual, this exercise will allow you to remove any obstacles in your path and to achieve inner freedom, which in turn will allow you to create greater freedom in all aspects of your life.

WHAT IS FREEDOM TO YOU?

The first step towards understanding and experiencing freedom is for you to decide what kind of freedom you are looking for. What does freedom mean to you? Do you equate it with having lots of money? Does freedom come from having a stable relationship? Do you have freedom if you can do anything you want and not be concerned about the outcome? Is freedom political, sexual, religious, or dependent upon the times in which you live?

Perhaps freedom for you would be relief from obligations and responsibilities in your life which feel like burdens. But think carefully about this, for it is easy to blame our obligations when the problem is actually the way we feel about them. We all live within society, and this involves responsibilities. We have jobs, families and communities which create structure in our lives and which give us our commitments and obligations. Sometimes we take for granted all that is precious within these structures. At other times we feel our burdens are too heavy, we suffer from stress and become ill. Then we wish away the things that, in better times, we value.

In these circumstances freedom is not to be found in relieving ourselves of our responsibilities; this is simply a way of changing our lives or reshaping the structures. Freedom is to be found in the way we feel about these responsibilities and in the way we carry them. If we carry them lovingly, lightly and with joy, never taking them for granted, then they are not burdens. If you know that you are undertaking your life's responsibilities because you choose to, then you know that you are free. When we discover the inner beauty and thought energy of the structures and obligations in our lives, then we transform them and we become happy. So freedom for you may lie in finding a way to experience joy in your life, even in the humdrum and burdensome aspects of it.

In the Bön view what matters is how free you feel yourself to be. To understand this you first need to be honest about what you want to be free from. This will give you information about what is holding you back in life. It may be an emotion, a person or a situation. The important thing is to know what it is, because the obstructions you have in your life are the keys to freedom and will point the way forward for you.

Below are some of the questions that you can ask yourself if you wish to develop an understanding of what may be holding you back from freedom.

- Do you feel controlled by your emotions or by circumstances in your life?
- Do old problems that you thought you had dealt with keep coming back?

- Do you suffer from a broken heart that you find hard to heal?
- Do you live in fear of losing your partner or children?
- Do you become scared easily by world events?
- Do you worry about money?
- Do you feel lonely?
- Are you grieving for yourself, or the death of a loved one?
- Do you feel thwarted by life in your attempts to be successful?
- Do you feel controlled by anger, or jealousy?
- Do you fear death?
- Do you fear poverty?
- Do you fear failure?
- Do you fear success and the experience of love?

These feelings and fears were as common in ancient Tibet as they are for us in the modern world. If you answered yes to one or more of these questions, as many of us would, then your inner personal freedom is restricted. The questions that are relevant to you will indicate where the restrictions lie. Fear, grief, anger, jealousy, regret and anxiety can all block the path to inner freedom. Once you have identified what is holding you back you can use the exercise for Awakening the Five Protectors to clear the obstacles and find inner freedom.

THE FOURTEEN TYPES OF FREEDOM

These fourteen freedoms were agreed by Bön Masters 1800 years ago, in AD 300, after 200 years of meditations. The Masters asked themselves what would be needed for each one of us to live happily in the material world. They knew that not everyone can be a great spiritual master, but that everyone can achieve spiritual and material happiness. These fourteen freedoms are about putting your house in order, seeing to all your needs and making sure that every area of your life is developed.

To fulfil all fourteen of the freedoms is considered a lifetime achievement. Most of us have some and not others. Look for the one that you feel you are most lacking and begin by working on this one. All fourteen freedoms can be developed using the thought exercise that follows them, Awakening the Five Protectors. Use this exercise to develop the freedom you most need, then you can move on, in time, to develop others.

These are the fourteen freedoms:

1. Financial freedom
2. Emotional freedom
3. Intellectual freedom
4. Freedom from negative individuals
5. Sexual freedom
6. Political and physical freedom
7. Freedom to choose what you eat
8. Freedom to educate your children as you wish
9. Freedom to hold any spiritual beliefs
10. Freedom from pain, anger and suffering
11. Freedom to live your own life as you see fit
12. Freedom to know that you can change your life as you think best
13 Spiritual freedom that makes your life work
14 Freedom that you understand and cherish

1 FINANCIAL FREEDOM

This form of freedom enables you to do many things and to have many choices. It is the kind of freedom that most people want, as they think it will solve all their problems. It won't, of course, but it can bring many benefits.

However financial freedom, no matter how important it seems, is relevant only to a small part of your life. There is nothing wrong with seeking such freedom, but never allow yourself to identify yourself with it, or you will become trapped by it and lose the opportunity to find true inner freedom, which is far more valuable.

2 EMOTIONAL FREEDOM

Emotional freedom means being free to feel whatever you want, to accept feelings as they arise and to follow impulses. So often we feel constrained by judgements and rules about our emotions: 'I mustn't feel angry', 'I should be over the grief', 'I hate feeling sad'. Without these constraints we are free to feel what we feel, with acceptance and peace.

However, emotions as thought energies have limitations, and can only carry us so far. They belong to the reactive world of the everyday mind and they can be addictive. If they are used in an addictive way then you no longer have emotional freedom.

Emotions are most valuable when they are steps to wisdom, when we learn from them and move on to greater levels of freedom, using the intellect. The freedom you can experience from emotions helps you to understand the nature of your own humanity, and that of others. By discovering the intensity, depth and quality of your emotions you will become aware of your capacity for feeling, and in turn for intellectual freedom.

Marshall was a rich man, with all the material possessions he could want and a lifestyle envied by many. He had a successful business, travelled to wonderful places and drove expensive cars.

But inside Marshall felt fractured and lonely. His relationships with others were blocked by mistrust, and he had never felt truly able to trust anyone. This was something that had been passed on to him by his father, who always feared that people were after his money, and it was a burden that kept Marshall isolated and trapped. He didn't feel free to open up, to love, to connect with others or to be himself. Marshall needed to find the second freedom, emotional freedom.

After Marshall came to see me and we talked he began to realise how little he knew about himself. He began the Awakening the Five Protectors exercise and asked the protectors to remove the emotional obstacles in his path.

After six months Marshall began to notice changes in his life. People were more open with him, they smiled, laughed and talked to him in a way that hadn't happened before. He realised that it was he who was behaving differently; others were simply responding. Marshall found himself making friends and learning to trust others. He learned that by being more open and trusting he was able to attract people who liked him for himself, not for his money.

By learning to trust Marshall brought meaning and value to his wealth. He began using it to help others and a year later he fell in love with a wonderful woman and got married.

3 INTELLECTUAL FREEDOM

Intellectual freedom is not just the right to say what we think in public without fear of recrimination, nor is it the right to think as we see fit. Intellectual freedom is far more than just academic freedom. It involves knowing the mechanism and structures of how we think in the everyday world, so that this material world will do what we instruct it to. In this sense it is the lifeblood of everyone's contribution to the society in which they live and is one of the most powerful, exciting and valuable freedoms possible. It involves mental discipline, effort and exploration, but once achieved it is the basis of satisfaction and happiness in life.

4 FREEDOM FROM NEGATIVE INDIVIDUALS

When negative energy is directed towards us by others, through their behaviour or language, we can feel that all our freedoms have been repressed. The world has many examples of negative people trying, directly or indirectly, to control or suppress the freedoms of others. This can happen via relationships, at work, within families, on the street – in fact in any situation. Sometimes it can take us completely by surprise and we can feel that we have been dumped on by others. Whether it is someone we know or a stranger, being on the receiving end of someone else's negativity is unpleasant and often shocking.

To achieve freedom from such negativity it is necessary to protect oneself using skilful thought energy. The Awakening the Five Protectors thought exercise will help you to achieve this.

You can't stop negative individuals from sending out their negativity, but you can choose not to receive it or to be affected by it, and when this happens you are free.

5 SEXUAL FREEDOM

The Western idea of sexual freedom is most commonly depicted as the freedom to experiment sexually with multiple partners. Sexual liberation, when it arrived with the Pill a few decades ago, brought the barriers crashing down and the 'permissive' age arrived, with sex happening younger, more often and with more partners than during the previous era.

The Tibetan Bön notion of sexual freedom is entirely different. This freedom is the discovery of rapture, unity and joy shared with a partner in a balanced and stable relationship.

All human beings instinctively have a deep longing for the coming together of our sexual energies and those of our souls. Sex at its most powerful and spiritual level can be an act of devotion and adoration, the most profound intimacy and the deepest connection two humans can have.

Through the arousal and transformation of sexual desire in the body, spirituality can be activated, developed and understood. Sexuality that is imbued with sacred intent can have a special appeal for people who long for spiritual growth and who also take great pleasure in earthly delights. Over the last twenty years, the Eastern practices of Tantra have become widely known and have been associated with sexuality and sexual practice. Sex actually plays a very small part in Tantra, which teaches the individual how to transform sexual energies in a balanced way, as a fast track to enlightenment. In the Tantra there are strict rules on morality and ethics and working and living with your mutually chosen partner. It also encourages sexual behaviour free from lust, greed and anger.

Tantra and other paths of sexually orientated spirituality teach us to respect and nurture the body as a holy place where spirituality and sexuality merge. The tantric way of thinking is to have unhurried lovemaking in which you learn to awaken all your senses and experience the depths and profundity of sexual thought energy. You let go of reasoning and habitual thinking, your body takes over and all routines of the ego are transformed into an expression of thankfulness for life and living.

In a similar way the Bön belief is that skilful sexual thought energies can help us to become physically less inhibited and morally more empowered so that we know the freedom of integrated and respectful sexual energy.

6 POLITICAL AND PHYSICAL FREEDOM

This freedom, which is abused and denied in so many parts of the world, starts and ends with you and the way you think about your neighbourhood, your country and the planet. Any political system begins as a string of thought energies put together to make a greater structure of thought energies.

You know that you have this freedom when you are able to contribute to and influence events that happen in your community, using skilful actions and thought energy. The outcome of something as mundane as the planning of a local parking scheme can be influenced by each individual. Your contribution must always be based on the good of all, not simply what you want out of it. Wishing for a better parking space for yourself alone is, in Bön terms, unskilful. Wishing for the best possible outcome for all those needing to park is skilful. Political freedom is therefore far more than just choosing who to vote for. It is the responsibility of all to ensure that the community is well cared for and is just and honest.

Physical freedom, which goes hand in hand with political freedom, is also about your contribution to freedom for all. If any one person is unjustly imprisoned, then it is for all of us to use skilful thought energy to help free them.

7 FREEDOM TO CHOOSE WHAT YOU EAT

You might well wonder what choosing what you eat has to do with freedom. It actually has a great deal, since people discovered the concepts of profit and control. In today's world those who control what you eat through distribution and marketing not only make huge amounts of money but also indirectly influence your health, and the health of your children, as well as the health of the food chain around the world.

Food, according to Bön wisdom, holds thought energies within it. So each time you eat you fill yourself not only with the food but also with the thought energy of the grower, distributor, shop, supermarket, factory farm, or organic farmer involved in its production and arrival on your table.

Therefore, the freedom to choose what to eat is not only a matter of taste but also a matter of awareness. You must become aware of what you eat, where it comes from, the way you eat, the attitudes you have to food and the predominant thought energies that arise within you at mealtimes.

You have the power to decide what type of food you want to consume and why. Choosing food that contains positive thought energy, that is, wholesome, nutritious food which is produced without chemicals and without harm to anyone, will help you to develop skilful thought energies in other areas of your life.

George had been sick for some years and he felt trapped by his body and his illnesses. Eventually he became bedridden and fell into a deep depression, feeling that he had no freedom to do anything or to become anything. Life was a prison and he didn't have the key to escape.

It was George's wife who came to me, asking for help. She had been caring for him for some years and she felt that, without help, he would simply give up on life completely. He was already painfully thin, having lost interest in eating along with everything else.

It was clear to me that George was suffering from allergies to many of the foods he was eating, which were filled with chemicals and additives. I taught George the Awakening the Five Protectors exercise and asked him to do it daily for a week, as his need was so great. I also asked him to begin a nutritious, wholefood diet filled with fresh fruit and vegetables.

With his wife's help George performed the exercise and began the new eating plan and found to his amazement that within days his physical and mental pain was diminishing. Soon he was pain-free and his vitality began to return. Within a week he was able to leave his bed and within a month he was able to go for a short walk to the local shops.

Within three months George had started to put on weight and was regaining his interest in life. Soon afterwards he found part-time work he could do from home and he was able to play with his children and to share the running of the house with his wife.

Doing the exercise and choosing to eat pure, nutritious foods gave George back his health, one of the most important freedoms there is.

8 FREEDOM TO EDUCATE YOUR CHILDREN AS YOU WISH

The education of our children starts with the way we conceive them and the way they are treated, spiritually, emotionally and physically as they are being born and immediately afterwards. The first thing they learn when they are in the womb is that they are loved, they contain a divine spark; they are nature's reminder that life is in all things.

As each child is born, according to Bön tradition, all of us are reborn, for the value of each life shapes all future life. Birth is a salutation of family and living and a recognition of the thought energies of the natural world. Through birth, all relationships are honoured. Birth creates opportunities, coupled to all existence and links that went before it.

In the Bön culture the child is assured key importance because the birth of the child has developed from personal understanding, inborn knowledge and the awareness and experience of the blessed and divine in all things, not just from the parents but also from everyone who was involved. As the child grows he or she not only has the love of the mother, but also the daily involvement of the father, family and neighbourhood.

The Bön moral principles guiding the education of children are these:

1 Parents do not own their children. A child comes to its parents as a result of the causes and effects of the parents' thought processes. The child receives its intellectual abilities from its mother and its spiritual and emotional abilities from its father. The parents' job will simply be to help it to unfold.

2 The child does own the parents. In this sense the parents are the servants of the child. Not to be pushed around or dominated, but to offer wisdom, advice and guidance along with love and respect.

3 The child should be encouraged to be as independent as possible from the earliest age. Whatever a child can do for itself it should be allowed to do. The child should also be taught to think independently.

4 The child should be given material resources as early as possible. By this it is meant that it should learn about handling money, growing food, using tools and developing practical skills such as sewing, caring for animals and cooking.

All external forms of education, such as schools and the like, help with social skills and learning what it takes to live within the structures of today's world, but, even at their best, they do not educate the inner thought energies of our children. As parents it is our responsibility, privilege and honour to do this. Through our help, our children can grow to become independent and free-minded about the choices and lifestyle they will eventually make for themselves. By approaching all our children born, unborn, growing and grown up in this way our children can reclaim the divinity within and the goodness in their daily living.

9 FREEDOM TO HOLD ANY SPIRITUAL BELIEFS

Spiritual beliefs enable people to find a way to the best and most uplifting parts of their character. Every person needs spiritual beliefs in order to lead a rounded and balanced life. And the freedom to choose those spiritual beliefs, as long as you cause no harm to others, is a fundamental right. People have been persecuted throughout history for their religious and spiritual beliefs. But in truth your beliefs will always be your own and unassailable. No one can tell you what to believe.

The freedom to believe what you choose is precious. But it is only of real value if you become a good person. This doesn't mean following a set of rules or laws laid down as part of a doctrine. It means actually getting in touch with your own goodness. This is truly earth-shattering when it happens because you discover just how wonderful you really are as both a human and a spiritual being.

In order to get in touch with your own goodness you need only sit quietly for a few minutes and focus on your own heart. Allow all your worries and anxieties to dissolve into your heart and you will feel your own goodness, bubbling away in your heart, ready to emerge.

10 FREEDOM FROM PAIN, ANGER AND SUFFERING

Anger, pain and suffering are all closely linked. Anger is born of pain and suffering and it also causes them. And when you are angry most of the time, or in pain most of the time, then you are suffering and not living. Freedom comes when you understand what causes your suffering, what contributes to the pain in your life and why you are angry. Through this understanding you can begin to stop suffering and start living.

Anger can become a habit which pollutes your thought energy. Anger is simply unskilful wisdom and it needs to be transformed into skilful wisdom. To do this repeat the exercise used for the ninth freedom. Sit quietly and focus on your heart. Feel your anger dissolving in your heart and as it dissolves you will feel your own skilful wisdom emerging.

The cure for anger, pain and suffering lies in the way you think and in the thought energy that you feed your identity. Instead of conditioning your everyday mind to anger, pain and suffering, you can condition it to joy and wisdom.

Hamish appeared healthy and successful, but underneath he was in turmoil and despair because he felt constant pain. He had been to one medical expert after another, attempting to find out what was wrong with his back, where the pain was. None could help him, all his tests proved clear and he feared he would spend the rest of his life in pain.

When he came to see me we quickly discovered that anger was the cause of his pain. Sometimes when anger is held in the body, unexpressed, for a long time, it appears as pain in an attempt to be recognised.

Hamish was able to tell me the cause of his anger almost straight away. He had been brought up to believe that anger was wrong and had never been allowed to express any anger at all. This, of course, had led to a build-up of anger in him which he never allowed himself to acknowledge. Hamish needed the tenth freedom, to release himself from anger, pain and suffering.

I asked Hamish to do the Awakening of the Five Protectors

and to ask them to help him transform his anger and pain into more skilful and creative thought energies.

At first Hamish felt an eruption of anger. As he did so he saw clearly how his anger had poisoned his mind, body and life. His anger began to dissolve and he felt a new sense of vitality. Within three months of starting the exercise all his pain had disappeared and Hamish felt his life was transformed. He discovered a new sense of creativity in himself and began writing a novel, which was eventually a great success.

11 FREEDOM TO LIVE YOUR OWN LIFE AS YOU SEE FIT

Most of us live within the structure of a society which lays down rules and customs for us to follow. Therefore true freedom to live our own lives as we see fit comes from learning about our inner resources and wisdom and our capabilities.

In the Tibetan Bön culture there were and are ways of assessing your own independence. I have often encouraged people I have worked with to do these things, as they reveal a great deal about our level of inner resources and self-determination.

- Spend a month in the wilderness on your own. Organise this safely and with common sense.
- Give something that is of importance to you to a less fortunate person.
- Serve the poor for one month. Live as they live.
- Work with the dying. Learn how to understand death.
- Work with the mentally ill.
- Work with children who have learning and behavioural problems.
- Look at all the excess belongings in your life and get rid of them.

- Examine the lifestyle you have built for yourself. Is it really who you are?
- Discover the strongest influence upon the way you live.
- Consider that you may know nothing at all and what you think you know has no basis.

Choosing one or more of these options to follow for a few weeks will reveal to you a great deal about yourself. It's easy to create a lifestyle based on the things you aspire to have, rather than who or what you aspire to be. These challenges can help you examine your inner lives to see if they support who you really are. In order to live your life in the way that you want you need to know what it is that you want and how to create skilful thought energy to support yourself.

12 FREEDOM TO KNOW THAT YOU CAN CHANGE YOUR LIFE AS YOU THINK BEST

Many people feel powerless to change their lives. But this is never true; we can all change our lives if we really want to. Freedom lies in knowing that this is always possible and that the life we are living is our choice.

Are you settling for a life that is not truly fulfilling? Are you allowing yourself to be satisfied with less because you believe you can't have anything more? Are you setting yourself goals which are too easy to reach and don't challenge your spirit?

If so then you need to know that change is possible and is up to you. It is in our most skilful thoughts that the real insights and actions for change lie. What we think and believe can happen is what we will create in our lives. To achieve this freedom you must let go of limiting beliefs which hold you back and keep you stuck. There is powerful life within you, waiting to be accessed and lived.

This freedom is closely linked with the next two. All three

together will allow you to feel a strong and very real sense of inner freedom.

Bruce never trusted himself to make decisions or to have respect for his own opinions and judgements. He felt as though everything in his life simply 'happened' to him and he was powerless to change anything or choose his own direction. As a result Bruce was unhappy with a lot of things in his life. He didn't particularly like his job, as a business administrator, he didn't like his home, a small apartment in a rough area of London, and he didn't even really like his girlfriend, who made endless demands and bullied him a lot.

Bruce was a victim of his own unskilful thoughts. There was no reason he could not change any of these things. All that stopped him was his own limiting beliefs, which were creating a self-made prison.

When Bruce came to see me he was thirty-three, a young, intelligent, good-looking man who nevertheless felt his life was permanently stuck in a rut. It was clear that Bruce needed to develop the twelfth freedom, the freedom to know that you can change your life as you think best. As we talked Bruce began to identify the beliefs that were holding him back. He believed that he did not deserve happiness, that he should settle for what he had and that he was not particularly talented or skilled.

Using the Awakening of the Five Protectors exercise Bruce began to dissolve these unhelpful beliefs and to awaken the freedom that he needed. He was hesitant at first and it took him some weeks to feel more confident in doing the exercise. But as he gained in confidence and stuck with it he began to see results.

As Bruce felt his ability to make changes grow so his excitement and energy grew. All the energy he had used to hold himself back from life was released and he was able to pour this energy into making positive changes.

Within six months Bruce had a new apartment, a new job, running a sports centre and had ended his unhappy relationship. The last time I saw him his eyes sparkled and his head was high. Even the way he walked had changed. He told me that he now knew he could do anything he chose with his life.

13 SPIRITUAL FREEDOM THAT MAKES YOUR LIFE WORK

Spiritual freedom is a powerful thought energy which, when accessed, will enable you to shape your life in the way you choose. Spiritual freedom is available in many forms and is all around you at all times. Yet many people don't know it is there, and don't allow themselves to receive it.

Here is a guide to opening up to spiritual freedom. Consider each point carefully.

- What part does love play in your life? Does it motivate you and teach you? Can you receive love in a spiritual way?
- Do you know that spiritual freedom is in everything, even things that disgust you?
- All you need to do to receive this freedom is to ask your inner self.
- Do not be caught up in prejudice or rumours, gossip or deceit. These unskilful thought energies block spiritual freedom and stop your life from working.
- Keep things simple in your life.
- Have fun, but never at the expense of other people.
- Be thankful for all the events in your life, both good and bad.
- Spend ten minutes a day in silence.

Take these guidelines with you as you go about your daily life and you will begin to notice and to connect with spiritual freedom. The more this happens, the more you will feel that your life is working in the way you want it to.

Melinda felt that her life was in a dead-end and that there was no future. She worked in a bank and didn't particularly enjoy it. She felt empty and as though everything she did was pointless. At twenty-nine she was a kind and thoughtful young woman, but she felt she had lost her way in life.

After meeting Melinda I felt that what she lacked was a spiritual element in her life. She had all her basic material needs taken care of, but the emptiness she felt indicated a spiritual gap. Melinda had been a member of a church, through her parents, but had given up going, as it meant very little to her.

Melinda began the Awakening the Five Protectors exercise and asked the protectors to remove the emptiness and futility from her life. As she continued with the exercise on a weekly basis she began to recognise the hole in herself that needed filling and her longing for spiritual fulfilment. Melinda began to explore more options and discovered that she had a great capacity for spiritual healing. Over the next two years she became a spiritual healer and teacher and she was invited to run workshops in the bank where she once worked as a clerk.

Melinda found the thirteenth freedom, spiritual freedom to make your life work. Through her spiritual beliefs she brought her life into balance and made it work. Today, ten years on, Melinda is a mature, fulfilled and deeply spiritual woman who has a positive effect on all who meet her. She loves what she does and she feels a profound inner sense of freedom which affects everything she does.

14 FREEDOM THAT YOU UNDERSTAND AND CHERISH

To begin to understand the nature and value of your own inner freedom, meditate upon the two statements below, allowing them to enter into you and absorbing them.

Freedom celebrates the beauty of your soul.

You are sacred. You are purity. You are all possibilities.

As you meditate quietly upon them these statements will begin to unlock the qualities of freedom within you. They will become a living part of your daily experience. Use this inner focus as a means to let this inner freedom emerge from within you. As your sense of freedom grows you will be filled with the purest thought energy and will feel empowered to make your life the way you want it to be.

THE FIVE PROTECTORS

Bön teaches that there are five protectors that live within your body throughout your life. Each of them is a minor god-force or deity, known as Lha. They are supercharged thought energies which have great influence over your life, supporting your vitality and good fortune. When they are out of balance then problems in your health and lifestyle occur.

The first is called the god of life, Srog Lha, and this god energy lives in your chest. Srog Lha can protect you from mental, physical and spiritual poverty. This thought energy directs and regulates all your vitality and senses. Your connection to life, personality and sense of adventure comes from Srog Lha.

The second is called the Yul Lha or the god of the place, which means your home, family identity and neighbourhood, as well as your country. This god energy lives in the crown of your head. Yul Lha grants wishes, peace, health and happiness. This thought energy influences where you live, the work you do and the friends you keep. Yul Lha is very affected by the atmosphere of places; it influences people's psychic and empathic abilities and their ability to care for others and to feel passionate about their home, neighbourhood, community and nationality.

The third is called Mo Lha, the god of females, and she lives in the right armpit. Mo Lha protects your life. This thought energy has guided you from birth, and grants a long and prosperous life. Mo Lha influences the duration of your life and its quality, as well as your ability to provide for yourself all your basic needs. Mo Lha also influences the conception and birth of children, your children until they become adults, female health and the way you relate to women and feminine energy. Healing, wisdom and insight are influenced by this thought energy as well as gardening, the kitchen and food. She can give the power to fight against injustices concerning your family and she also influences musical talent and can help to connect you to any kind of artistic abilities.

The fourth is called Pho Lha, the god of males, and he lives in your left armpit. Pho Lha protects you against physical illness and mental pain and removes obstacles. This thought energy brings courage and determination to everything you do. Pho Lha helps men to deal with their fears and emotions and stops violence between men but can also be awakened to help with mental or physical defence. Protective when needed, this thought energy develops freedom of fear of physical conflict.

The fifth is called the god of enemies, the Dgra Lha, and lives on your right shoulder. Dgra Lha protects you from enemies and negativity. It keeps you safe from harm and can deal with any problem. In addition, this thought force, although compelling and immensely powerful, is gentle but unswerving, and helps you to increase success and influence. When you feel that you have nowhere to turn, Dgra Lha creates opportunities for sudden and unexpected help.

You Are All of the Five

All these five god-forces live within every human being, waiting to be woken from their dormant state and integrated into our lives. They are part of us and at the same time they are particular and profound thought energies that have specific functions within the emotional, intellectual and physical experiences of our lives.

If we do not consciously develop them then these powerful thought energies will only ever be activated by the demands of sudden circumstances or crises, and the vast bulk of their power will go to waste. They can become weak or strong, depending upon your lifestyle and the extent to which you have developed your inner life.

By choosing to develop them you can heal and balance your life and create the freedom that you need. They are gateways to freedom and will transform any obstructions, allowing you to become free in body, mind and spirit.

Awakening the Five Protectors

This profound and powerful thought energy exercise can be used to awaken each of the five protectors and to remove any obstacle you feel lies in the way of your freedom, including ill health. It is the key to inner freedom and to creating positive change in your life and to regaining essential vitality that has been lost through unskilful behaviour, thoughts, or unexpected circumstances. In performing the exercise you will increase your life force and your capacity to attract positive life energy. Before you begin it is important to prepare yourself. Be aware of the fourteen freedoms and the one that you relate to most powerfully and wish to bring into your life. As you focus upon this, thinking about the feelings it evokes in you, allow it to create ideas and information within you.

Based on an ancient Bön ritual, the exercise is best done once a week in the early morning just after sunrise. If this is not possible then choose a time that feels right to you. Do the exercise first for yourself, and later, if you wish, you can do it for family and friends. You must follow the instructions exactly if the exercise is to be effective. It is completely safe and will begin to show its effects almost immediately.

STEP ONE

Clear a space on a table or on the ground. Make sure it is clean. Then spread a white cloth out on the surface. Place five small white bowls as in the diagram below:

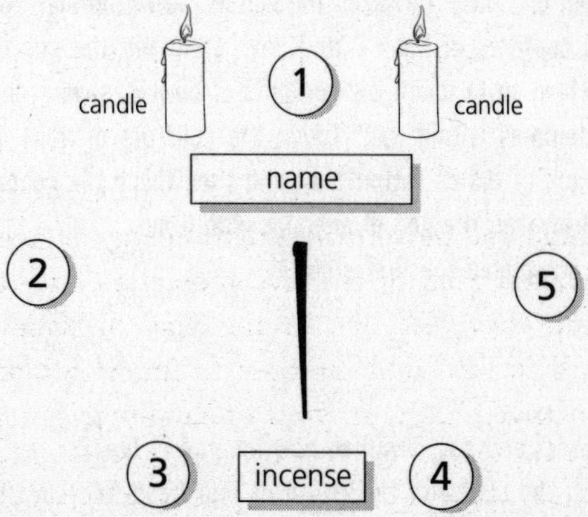

Into bowl 1 pour a little fresh water. This is the symbol of Srog Lha.

Into bowl 2 pour some fresh milk, the symbol of Yul Lha.

Into bowl 3 place a little of any grain such as rice, barley or wheat; add to this something precious of yours, to symbolise Mo Lha.

Into bowl 4 put some salt to symbolise Pho Lha.

Into bowl 5 put any type of foodstuff that you like the taste of to symbolise Dgra Lha.

To the left and to the right of number 1 place one small candle in each of the marked squares. These candles will allow your skilful thoughts to radiate though the atmosphere.

On the square between 3 and 4 place incense of your choosing. The incense will help you to create clear and powerful thoughts.

In the centre of the circle copy the Tibetan symbol as in the diagram on to the white cloth with a red pen. Then above it write your complete name, also in red.

Now you are ready to proceed.

First, light the incense. Then the candles left to right. Then write in your name again and draw the symbol below your name; this is regarded as holding your attention to the earth with a spike of powerful and indestructible thought energy.

Now with the forefinger of your right hand touch the contents of bowl 1. Say quietly but out loud, 'I awaken the god of life within me.' Then move on to touch the contents of bowl 2 and say, 'I awaken the god of the place within me.' Move on to touch the contents of bowl 3, saying, 'I awaken the goddess of females within me.' Touch the contents of bowl 4, saying, 'I awaken the god of males within me,' and then touch the contents of bowl 5 and say, 'I awaken the god of enemies within me.'

You have completed the first step.

STEP TWO

Touch your chest and say, 'Awaken now the god of life.'

Next, touch the centre of the crown of your head and say, 'Emerge, the god of the place.' Now, touch the middle of your right armpit and say, 'Emerge, the goddess of females.' Now, touch the middle of your left armpit and say, 'Emerge, the god of males.'

Now, with a forceful action with the palm of your hand, slap the right shoulder and say in a loud, commanding voice, 'Wake up from your sleep, the god of enemies!'

At this point clap your hands as loud as you can and with force, five times. Clapping awakens dormant thought energies. As you do so, say the following: 'Together find your place. Let the god of life take charge, directing the others so that each shall release their knowledge to me and show me their power, so I may transform all obstructions into freedom. As they are part of me so I create these five!'

Now visualise a burst of white lights flashing brilliantly from your chest and flowing to the crown of your head, where it flashes the colour of sunlight. It moves to the centre of your right armpit, where it flashes emerald green and on to your left armpit where it flashes a deep blue, and then across to your right shoulder where it forms a sphere of pulsating purple light which sits upon your shoulder. Sit quietly and you feel the light moving from your chest, to the crown of your head, to your right armpit, then to your left armpit, then to the sphere on your shoulder. Let the light flow like this for a few minutes.

You are ready for step three.

STEP THREE

Now focus upon your name, written on the cloth. Write your name again, tracing over the letters you wrote earlier. Now into your name direct all the things that you want to change, so you can remove obstacles and achieve any freedom you choose.

From the purple sphere, send a ray of purple light into your name. Now say, 'God of life within me, instruct the god of enemies to destroy the obstructions within me and without that restrict my path to freedom.'

Breathe in through your nose and then out through your mouth slowly. Clap your hands. Now say, 'To each of the five awakened protectors within me I offer up these bowls that contain what you most desire. Enjoy the offerings of the bowls.'

When you have done this sit in quiet contemplation for a few moments. The exercise is completed.

The Divine in All Things

In the ancient tradition of the Northern Treasure School of Bön, everything is alive in the sense that it is naturally imbued with divine thought energies. In ancient times the Tibetans saw that the purpose of life was to make contact with all the elemental thought energies of the universe and planet. Everything, from the mountains to clouds, thunder, air, earth, our bodies and minds, is full of life-sustaining and life-giving thought energy.

It is as important now as then to come into contact with these thought energies and to derive energy, power, wisdom and joy while cultivating compassion. Each person now, as then, has the right and the ability to do this directly, in a beautiful and pure way, beginning with the Awakening of the Five Protectors.

In the Bön tradition a life in which the Five Protectors are not awoken and known is only half a life. By awakening them you create for yourself the opportunity to experience true inner freedom and the divine and natural energies in all areas of your life, for the rest of your days.

9

HELPING OTHERS

Skilful thought energy can be used to heal, help and create good fortune for other people. The Bön belief is that everything we do should be for the benefit of others as well as ourselves and that this should be the guiding intention of our lives, both in a general sense and specifically.

We help others by thinking for them, but this does not mean doing their thinking for them. It simply involves creating the right kind of thought energy to bring benefit for them. Skilful thinking for others connects you to the beauty and majesty of the human spirit. It is especially important to do it for people who have genuine difficulties and are confused or unable to help themselves.

ACTIVE COMPASSION

Informed and active compassion is the essence of thinking for others because it is thought energy designed to create benefits. Such active compassion means showing care and consideration for your fellow human beings and is the best thing you can do. It can overcome all prejudices and spread love around the world.

As you live your life with active compassion you learn how to craft, construct and apply miracles on a daily basis. These miracles are your thought energies releasing the inherent abundance and beauty of the life force of the planet and humanity.

BECOMING EMPATHIC

Empathy is to feel what another feels and to know why they feel as they do. Empathy is more than intuition, it is a dimension of our consciousness that can create solutions.

All of us have the ability to be empathic. To activate and develop your ability to feel empathy gives you awareness and knowledge of thought energy which will help you to understand the origins of things, and how and why people create their problems.

DEVELOPING EMPATHY THOUGHT EXERCISE

Rise early in the morning if you can, if not do this in a quiet time and place. Do the exercise for as long as it takes, no more than twice a month at first. In time you will need no more than twenty minutes to do it and will know when it is the right time to do it.

Standing with your feet slightly apart, gently stretch your arms above you and to the sides. Breathe in and out. Now feel energy flowing down through your hands and outstretched arms into your body and down your legs into your feet. From your feet the energy rises up again to your arms and out through your hands, spilling in a cascade of spirals around you and creating a white net of energy.

Slowly bring your arms down and your feet together and then sit on the floor. Now lie down on your back and see the white net hanging above you and around you. Start to hear a million voices talking quietly around you; they sound like the sea or wind in the trees.

Suddenly, you are in the minds of every living human being on this planet. The white net stretches out to each of them, while attaching itself to you.

You start to feel what they feel, and in addition to know why. Then you find your attention drawn to those people you know and have known and to your family members and friends. You feel what they feel and know why.

You now experience a great unfolding of compassion that travels like a tidal wave to all those you know and out to every other human being in existence. Rest for twenty minutes on the floor before getting up.

As you do this exercise you will find that you start to know things about people and how to help them. You will also gather spiritual knowledge and develop great insight, compassion and understanding.

WHEN TO HELP OTHERS

Helping other people requires care, timing, skill and the absence of ego. All of us have a natural desire to help other people, but often through lack of application we aren't aware of this desire. As you begin to help others then your wish to help and your understanding of who to help will become more focused and clear. If at all possible, when helping others first gain their permission. This makes the help you give very effective indeed. Sometimes circumstances stop you from doing this and in these cases it's best to tune in to the person with your thought energy. Often this happens very easily as you unconsciously connect with a friend or person in need.

The time to help someone is when they can't help themselves. That is, when they can't determine a course of action to take, when they are trapped by circumstances and don't know which way to turn or when they are prevented from taking action to help themselves.

Make sure, when helping others, that you are sending the kind of help they need, rather than the kind you would like to give. There can be a difference and it is important to be aware of it.

Often the best way to help someone is by allowing them to create their own solutions, while focusing your energy on helping to improve the general situation or their ability to create solutions. For instance, if someone is hurt and angry about a demotion at work, you could send helping energy to the working and creative areas of their life, while leaving them to solve the immediate problem.

Here's a checklist to help you recognise when, and when not to help others.

Help a person when:

- They are not in control of their circumstances.
- They are not in control of their mental or physical health.
- They have lost their means of living, through no fault of their own.
- They have lost someone they love, or their sense of security.
- A person experiences a loss of faith, in religion, an ideal, or a person, or when someone finds it hard to trust, but seeks to trust.
- An individual stands up to protect the freedoms of others.
- A person is seeking to improve their life and circumstances.
- A person is seeking a spiritual or creative dimension to their life.
- A child or innocent person is in trouble.

Don't help when:

- A person squanders wealth and resources recklessly.
- A person abuses the trust of others to improve their own situation.
- A person steals the emotions, energy, belongings or property of others.
- A person commits acts of violence towards other people.

- A person needs to face up to profound truths about their personality and lifestyle.
- Someone seeks to diminish other people to make themselves feel better or seeks revenge for any reason.
- Someone refuses to help themselves because they feel that others should do things for them.
- A person ignores the opinions and feelings of others or believes that they are superior to other people.
- People gossip, cause mischief or seek harm of any kind towards others.
- People refuse to help less fortunate people than themselves.

The best long-term way to help someone is by directing liberating thoughts to their situation in order to dissolve any obstacles or problems. The individual will then experience a change of consciousness, happiness and direct empowerment.

HELPING EFFECTIVELY

Occasionally you will come across someone who seeks help simply in order to be noticed and who is unwilling to help themselves. Such people tend to drain your personal energy and any help you give them is unlikely to be effective. The best way to deal with them is to direct towards them the thought energy of unconditional love and the desire for self-knowledge.

Unskilful desires to help people can also cause problems. In order to help people it is important to know yourself first and to deal with your own problems. Helping others because it makes you feel good, or needed, is not appropriate. If you help others just to make yourself feel better then your good intentions will lose their potency and the person you tried to help will not gain much benefit. Help because people need it and because you have the ability to give to others.

If someone asks you for help then think carefully before you agree. Look beyond their words and decide for yourself whether it would be right, or possible, to help them. Don't simply do as they ask, think about what kind of help would be most effective. Ask yourself whether the person has a plan for helping themselves, and if they do, whether it is a good plan or is simply adding to their problems. To help a fellow human being takes compassion, wisdom and common sense. Before you rush to the aid of anyone, be sure of the other person and sure of yourself.

PROTECTING YOURSELF

In helping other people you involve yourself in their problems and their life. In order to avoid situations that you may not be able to deal with or that you shouldn't be involved in, you need to develop a protection and filtering system. To do this you must detach yourself from the situation and assess it before you get involved, judging carefully when and how it is right to help.

Develop compassion and love towards others and you will automatically come into contact with those you can help. But there will always be situations where to rush in and help is to get yourself into difficulties. So use discernment. If you act with love then you will develop insight and you will easily be able to distinguish between those who simply want to use you or gain attention and those who genuinely need help.

TRUSTING YOUR INSTINCT

There may be moments in your life when you get a gut feeling that someone you know needs your help. When this happens, direct as much good, helping thought energy as you can towards them.

Even if it turns out that the person actually seemed fine, it may have been their unconscious energies crying out for help.

It could also have been that someone they know was in need of help and your friend unconsciously passed on this needy thought energy, because we all conduct other people's thought energy.

Always trust your instinct if you feel that someone needs help, whether you know them or not. Use love and compassion and be clear about what you want for them and about the end outcome you have in mind.

CREATING GOOD FORTUNE

In the Bön tradition the best type of good fortune there is starts with the heartfelt desire to create happiness for others. This desire will always support and protect you in hard times and bring you success and advancement in good times. Good fortune is not just to do with money and position, but with happiness, glad spirits and the sanctity of the human soul.

It is the happiness that comes from truly sharing yourself and offering freely what you have, knowing that it will return to you multiplied. When you create good fortune for others it is passed on. Good fortune is inclusive, not exclusive. There is always enough and plenty to share.

Directing Good Fortune

After you have created the thought energy of good fortune, you need to direct it. It helps if you can be as exact as possible in your direction of thought energy, especially in the early stages of developing your skill. As you become more proficient, then you will find your own way of directing things, but here I shall explain a tried and trusted method which has been refined over time.

This method of directing your thought energy is simple but very effective. It develops great vitality and mental sensitivity. Do it as often as you feel necessary.

- Always be in a relaxed and uncluttered state of mind before you start to direct good fortune.
- Feel the thought energies within you and around you that relate to compassion, good fortune and healing flow towards you. They stream in together, from within and without to join as a mass of thought energy.
- Picture in your mind the person that you wish to help, wherever they may be, even if they are sitting in front of you.
- At this point, start to place your particular beneficial thought into the mass of thought energy.
- As you focus upon it, it builds up power and potency.
- Breathe in and out. Clap your hands once.
- Send the ball of thought energy off to do the good things you have instructed it to do.

Andrew had a friend whose life had fallen to pieces. His friend was trapped in a foreign country, with no money, and the possible threat of imprisonment for a crime he had not committed. Andrew's friend thought he could sort things out on his own and had refused offers of help. But Andrew was deeply worried and wanted to do something to help get his friend through his troubles.

Andrew sat down and directed good fortune to his friend. He did this every day and within a few days his friend experienced a major change in his life, circumstances and spirit. He was freed and was able to return home. Only much later did Andrew's friend tell him that while in trouble he had dreamed that Andrew sent him good fortune and had felt sure that things would change.

SUSTAINING AND HEALING FRIENDS AND STRANGERS

Friends are people who once were strangers and whose thought energy fused with yours as you came together. Strangers are friends you have yet to know. Both are worthy of sustaining with healing and helpful thought energy.

This thought energy is useful for helping people, friends or strangers, get through difficult times. If I am walking in the street and I see a great sadness in a person passing by, I will often send them sustaining thought energy as it helps them to regroup their strengths and move forward. We should all try to help each other. Here is how to do it.

- Focus upon the person you wish to help.
- Focus upon the person's difficulties.
- See the connection between the difficulties and the mental energies of the person.
- Direct your thought energy to the connection, dissolving the problem and creating helpful energy from it.
- Now direct this energy to the person in the following ways:

1. Direct sustaining thought energy to the person's emotions.

2. Direct sustaining thought energy to the person's physical body.

3. Direct sustaining thought energy to the person's opportunities for material gain and independence.

This last point is very important. Thought energy that you direct inwards should always have a material 'pathway' to be expressed tangibly in the everyday world. Including this thought energy for material advancement and success will speed up and improve the person's chances of overcoming difficulties.

Tamara was fabulously wealthy and spoiled and she knew it. Although she enjoyed all the material goodies in her life and the fun of being a New York socialite, she wanted to do something really useful with her life. But she had no idea what.

I suggested that, while she was thinking about what to do, she try sustaining and healing others with good fortune, by generating love and kindness in her heart. Tamara began by directing healing energy towards people she knew were having problems. She then directed healing energy towards strangers, people she saw in the street and felt were unhappy.

In this way Tamara discovered that she had a gift for helping people overcome their problems. Friends told her their lives were turning around and that all kinds of good things were happening to them.

One day a woman she met at a party told her of her problems. Tamara directed good fortune and healing towards her over the next few days. Two months later she bumped into the woman, who told her of a miraculous change in her circumstances. Things had come about exactly as Tamara had hoped.

Tamara felt very humble and happy at discovering this potential in herself. She continued her efforts to help others and became a far more mature and spiritual person than she had been. She became a spiritual counsellor, giving help wherever she could and valuing her inheritance as a spiritual blessing.

HEALING YOUR FAMILY

Using thought energy to help and heal members of your family is quite different to using it for your friends, unless you regard a friend as a member of your immediate family. In order to be of real use to a family member you must put sentiment to one side.

Use this simple thought exercise, which can be applied to anything from illness to the shock of losing a job, the pain of separation and divorce or the anxiety caused by money problems. You can use it for yourself as well as for any family member.

Do the exercise three times a week until changes happen, which will normally be very soon.

First answer these questions:

- What type of suffering or problem does your family member have?
- Has it affected their personality?
- Has it affected their health?
- Do they get angry and tired at the same time?
- How does their situation make you feel about yourself?

Now bring all the answers you have found and any thoughts you have about the situation together in a structure or idea that you feel happy with and focus it in your mind. You might choose a shape, a colour or a picture.

Direct this composite thought to the family member. See it sitting on the top of their head, moving through their body and mind, cleaning it of all obstructions. When it gets to the feet and exits through their toes, the thought energy then comes back to you ready for attention. At this point, have in front of you a clean bowl that you can easily dispose of afterwards. Into this bowl, pour some fresh clean milk.

Now direct the absorbed negativities, ill health or unskilful thoughts or actions into the milk. Let the milk take on all the inner rubbish and blockages. Next strike a match or a lighter across the surface of the milk. Think of this fire destroying and purifying all the absorbed negative energy.

Clap your hands three times. Then carefully take the bowl of milk and pour it down the drain. Wash the milk down the drain with water. Then destroy the bowl, wrap it in a cloth and break it and throw it away, or if it is plastic or paper wrap it up and dispose of it.

Amanda was a full-time mother of four when her husband became seriously ill. The doctors didn't know what was wrong with him and her husband's employers, who had previously been friendly, became distant and difficult and refused to pay him while he was off sick.

Amanda at the time had a housekeeper, Roberta, who knew the thought exercise for healing and helping family. She taught it to Amanda, who focused on her husband, on herself, the children and the financial situation.

A few days later a doctor in Europe heard about Amanda's husband, agreed to see him and found that he had a rare genetic disorder. Three months later, her husband's company came through with all the money that was owed.

Months later Amanda's husband died. Amanda used the exercise to help her grief and to help her children cope with the loss.

Amanda had never had to look after herself before and didn't know how she would support her family. One morning over a cup of coffee, she and Roberta were talking about things they liked to do to relax. Roberta liked to bake. Amanda never had. So they did some then and there.

Weeks later the two of them went into business, opening a wholefood bread and cake shop. They now own several shops and Amanda has discovered that she is an excellent businesswoman. She and Roberta still use the exercise to solve problems in their family lives.

CREATING GOOD FORTUNE FOR YOUR FAMILY

Helping a family member to find a job, a friend, abundance or general happiness is an easy thing to do using thought energy, but once again you must be sure of your intentions and make sure you are acting for the benefit of the family member, rather than yourself.

Do this exercise for seven days, starting on a Sunday. Repeat this three times.

Direct your thought energy to the person concerned, cleansing and purifying them of all blocks and obstructions. See or feel their obstructions being dissolved by your powerful and compassionate thought energy.

Now direct a ray of pure, white thought energy into their heart. This starts to awaken in them the positive energy that attracts good fortune. You are stimulating their vitality.

Next see them showered with money, offers of friendship, love and respect. See other people giving them good fortune and sharing their own vitality with your family member.

When you have finished this, clap your hands loudly seven times.

The person you are helping will now start to create their own first steps to good fortune through positive actions. They may help people, show kindness, or express compassion to those who are less fortunate than they are. As you continue with the exercise happiness and vitality will begin to occupy their mind, body and soul.

Kieran was very worried about his brother Patrick, who had suffered a series of troubles. Patrick, a business manager, had been made redundant for the second time in three years. He had a wife and two children to support and very little money. He was a talented, hard-working man, but his bad luck had made him feel a failure. Kieran worried that his brother might not find another job in his unhappy state of mind and wanted to help him.

He did the above exercise, sending good fortune to Patrick, for seven days. At the end of this time he saw his brother, who seemed much more cheerful. Kieran did the exercise for the second seven days, after which his brother phoned to tell him he had a couple of job interviews lined up.

A week after Kieran finished the third seven days of the exercise, Patrick phoned to tell him he'd landed a fantastic job. His brother sounded excited and happy and Kieran felt delighted.

HELPING CHILDREN

When helping children it is important to gain the parents' permission first, if at all possible.

Children can be helped with all kinds of problems, from illness to bullying, friendship problems, lack of confidence, aggression or shyness. With healing thought energy and the encouragement of caring adults children can become very adept at finding solutions.

Healing thought energy should be directed to the parent and the child at the same time. As you direct thought energy to the parent it will flow to the child, bringing protection and safety.

The thought energy that you direct to the child will start to attract positive situations and helpful opportunities. Thought energy, if directed with genuine intent to a child, will always bless and protect them, regardless of apparent circumstances or conditions.

A THOUGHT EXERCISE FOR HELPING CHILDREN

To help children in difficulties the following exercise is very effective.

Do it for four days, in the morning, between 5 a.m. and 9 a.m.

Close your eyes and send a warm, quiet wave of gentle thought energy to the feet and up to the head of the child. This wave of energy encompasses the child in a sphere, which then remains to ease and protect the child and drive away negative energies.

Now see the child's heart becoming a sky-blue light that pulses and permeates their body and mind. The child becomes connected to a constant stream of healing and happiness.

This gift will act as a protection throughout the child's life.

Isla was deeply upset when she heard that a friend's daughter was being badly bullied at school. The thirteen-year-old was becoming withdrawn and depressed and her parents were at their wits' end to know how to help. The school had intervened, but the girl felt that this only made things worse;

the bullies laughed at her for telling the teachers.

After asking permission from both the girl's parents, Isla used the thought exercise above to help her, sending healing to her and to her parents for four days.

A month later Isla saw the family again. She heard that three weeks earlier the girl had come to her parents and told them she had realised she was at the wrong kind of school. She explained that she wanted to move to a smaller school she had read about. The parents had investigated this and found there was a place for their daughter at the new school.

Three months later Isla heard that the girl was loving her new school, there was no bullying and she had made good friends.

HELPING THE WORLD

In the West, we often think of the third world as a separate and far more deprived area than our own prosperous countries. In fact, the entire planet is in a state of third world poverty and there is suffering and deprivation in all countries. We all know a great deal about the suffering in the world, in our own country and others. It is brought into our homes by the media and enters into our consciousness, spreading the intensity of the suffering.

If you wish to help alleviate the suffering of others in this world you can donate money, resources and your skills. You can also help using skilful thought energy.

DIRECTING LOVE THOUGHT EXERCISE

You can use this exercise for any kind of suffering, anywhere. It is powerful and intense and will help to alleviate the pain of others.

Simply tune into the thought energy of the suffering you witness and send love and compassion to those who suffer. Give them all the love you can, directing it to a group of people, a situation or a conflict and the love will start the healing.

As soon as you decide consciously to share your love and direct it to others it will be with them. Share and they will receive and out of this more resources and help will come.

HEALING AND HELPING

Using the immense power of thought energy you have the ability to help anyone who needs it, as well as to direct the flow of your own life.

You need never feel helpless or at the mercy of fate. You have within you all the resources you need to bring about change. Use your resources, and your great healing and helping ability, with care and respect. Never intrude into the lives of others, or force your ideas on anyone else. Help by sending others the power and the energy to choose their own course.

In the same way, you must always treat your own life with respect and patience. Healing does not always mean instant health or wealth; sometimes it means treading gently and learning through experience. Use your abilities wisely, and you will always make the right choices.

10

THE WORLD IN A SINGLE THOUGHT

In the previous chapters you have learned many aspects of the development and use of pure, skilful thought energy. This energy is profound, immediate and limitless. Such thought energy can become the illumination of humankind and the highest impulse of life. If you have come this far through the book then you are well on your path to becoming a truly skilful thinker, one of those men, women and children who understand that spiritual thought is more powerful than any material influence.

Now, in the final chapter of the book, I want to take you one step further, into the realms of consciousness.

Consciousness transcends our patterns of everyday thinking and reacting and gives us free will and the ability to think, in the truest sense, for ourselves. I will show you how it is possible to transcend your identity, that is, the everyday you, and connect with your own higher consciousness and spirituality. And in doing this you will become aware of the connections between all things in this world, and the oneness of all things, so that ultimately all that exists blends into a single, pure thought.

Within each of us is the pure thought energy of eternity. Wise, tranquil and filled with universal magnificence, it infuses every part of life, creating connections that lead to the profound experience of unity. This deep power of thought energy in which we exist, once discovered by each of us reveals our goodness. Through connecting with your consciousness you will move forward on the spiritual trail which we are all, ultimately, bound to follow.

IDENTITY

Before you can connect with your consciousness it is important to understand the nature of identity and the difference between identity and consciousness.

Our identity is the part of ourselves that we recognise and connect with every day. This part of us believes that our lives are all about responding to the demands of our immediate environment and the activities of our daily lives, such as going to work, getting sick or becoming well, organising and running our lives and raising our families. Nearly all the activities of our identity are routine and the skills developed by the identity are neither conscious nor unconscious, they are simply reactions to thoughts, feelings and events in our lives.

Identity creates memories of the past and interpretations of the present which enable us to live in the everyday world. Yet our belief in the truth of the conclusions of identity is misplaced; much of what identity presents us with is simply a false impression.

The identity believes that the difference between ourselves and others is the primary quality of human beings. The consciousness, however, knows that in fact the primary quality of humanity is its connection, through the power of skilful thought energy.

Whereas consciousness is permanent and unchanging, our identity changes all the time, because it is only the promoter of the conclusions that the mind has created. Yet the identity likes to believe that it is all-powerful, independent and in control.

The thought energy of identity is quite separate to the thought energy of consciousness. Conscious skilful thought energy enters the spiritual realm and illuminates all that we can be, while the identity is consumed with habitual thought patterns which belong to the everyday world and cannot enter the spiritual dimension.

The habitual thought patterns of the identity are not the essential us, yet most people believe that they are. And as long as we believe that habitual thinking embodies our utmost aptitude then we bind ourselves completely to the everyday world, for we cannot think our way into the spiritual reality using habitual thought. Reactive thought is essentially harmless. But it can separate us from our ability to be happy. Our reactive habit to accept as true, act upon and be caught up in anything that we identify with can restrict the development of our higher thought energies.

Consciousness is complete in itself. The identity suspects that there is more than just itself, but is afraid to find out. Yet as we begin to see through the shortcomings of our identity and to feel dissatisfaction with the dominance of everyday thinking, we begin to long for something more.

Habitual thinking stops us from connecting with reality and presents us, instead, with diversions and dead-ends. The unskilful thought energies of the identity travel wherever they wish to go, taking us round in circles. Only when we transcend the identity and reach consciousness can we choose our journey.

CONSCIOUSNESS

The exceptional attribute of the human mind that gives humanity its greatest qualities is consciousness. We see the world piece by piece through the eyes of our identity, yet the complete picture can only be found through reaching consciousness.

Our consciousness descends into us from the juncture where matter, pure thought energy and humanity meet. The Bön tradition says that consciousness flows from the brain to our emotions, feelings and thoughts. Then it moves out into the environment, where it sparks other people's consciousness. Consciousness and its use through skilful thinking helps you to understand the ways in which the majority of people think, while encouraging you still to be and live in the world.

Consciousness reveals the staleness and sparseness of habitual thinking, which is to do with acquisition, rather than understanding. It empowers us to think dynamically, embracing parallel connections between our mind, identity and consciousness.

Consciousness and its thought energy is radical, world-shattering, sometimes harsh and always awe-inspiring. This thought energy is uncompromising and can turn comfortable routine on its head. But it brings compassion, and can allow us to journey into our own deepest hells without fear or doubt.

The Tibetan Bön tradition suggests that most people only actually think truly conscious thoughts for about five minutes a year. The rest of the time is spent reacting to, and understanding the consequences. Major events in our lives, such as illness, loss and change often spark off such conscious thought, as we struggle to make sense of what has happened.

Thoughts that come out of consciousness not only give structure to the spiritual dimensions, but also bring the spiritual dimensions and the everyday world together.

Western science has made great strides in understanding what life is and how it evolved, yet in the search for understanding, knowledge and solutions to the world's problems, consciousness has been neglected by scientists and politicians alike.

Humanity is the greatest mystery facing science. Researchers may have a hint of what causes reasoning, recollection and wisdom, the workings of our body and certain aspects of brain chemistry, but they have no explanation for the one thing we all share – our consciousness.

Yet no scientific theory of the cosmos can be inclusive if it does not attempt to explain consciousness, for it is the only thing we can be certain of. The world and our entire lives may well be a false impression, a figment of our state of consciousness.

Western culture sees knowledge as something in the outside world, something to be tracked down and interpreted. The Bön view, however, is that knowledge lies inside ourselves. This is a concept many people in the West, trained always to look outside themselves, find difficult. Yet to reach and understand the nature of consciousness we must look inward, not outward. All you need to do to discover the origins of consciousness is to ask your soul.

TRANSCENDENCE

To transcend is to go beyond all the ordinary senses and impressions that we have in our body, identity and intellect, moving through the dimensions of consciousness, spurred on by the motivating power of compassion, towards a profound vision of how all things are interconnected. When you are able to transcend your identity and reach spiritual consciousness then you will experience the world bound together in a single, universal thought.

In transcendence you understand that everything comes from nothing and that nothing is not a void or emptiness, but an opportunity for consciousness to celebrate its connections. This celebration in turn creates life. Transcendence tell us that there is no here, there, now or then. Our identity creates these impressions so that we may have the life we need.

Here are the five steps necessary to transcend your identity and discover your own consciousness.

STEP 1 SUSPEND JUDGEMENT

Every day people judge one another and the events around them. This judgement, born of ignorance, creates poisonous thoughts which spread damage to those who judge as well as those who are judged.

People take dark pleasure in pronouncing judgements over others. Yet these unskilful thought energies create negativity and join together to become brooding and dangerous, influencing the minds of every individual upon this planet and wounding humanity.

Judgements by others or towards others restrict your ability to grow and be happy and will hold you back. Judgements over others are a ploy of the identity, to keep you anchored in the everyday world and far from consciousness. For true judgement, we must look to our inner selves and become our own judges. This is the only kind of judgement that is valid.

It is important for us to relate to other people in such a way that we only give and receive constructive thought energy. We owe this to others and to ourselves. We need to become more mindful and to increase our awareness in order to avoid making judgements or absorbing the judgements of others, which might trap us in unskilful thought energies, creating barriers and limitations.

Choose today to suspend judgement over others and to refuse to accept their judgements of you.

STEP 2 STRENGTHEN VIRTUE

In contrast to judgement there is virtue. It lies within all of us and is the observance of the natural order of the earth and our inner goodness. By observing the practice of virtue in all things we establish our integrity, which in turn brings pure thought energy into a state of conscious recognition in our lives.

As we observe virtue we look at ourselves in the light of pure thought energy and discover that our life is living beauty.

All things, the familiar, the good and the bad reveal their purpose in life. We gain understanding. No anger or misfortune can end our trust in this experience. The infinite thought energy of purity presents itself to us, giving us natural joy and constant bliss.

Discover your own capacity for virtue by becoming aware of the goodness within you.

STEP 3 REJECT THE SEVEN POLLUTIONS

These are expressions of unskilful thought energy which reduce our consciousness and slow us down on the path to insight and the experience of pure thought energy. See whether you identify with any of the seven and if so how these experiences influence and direct your life.

1 The fantasy that individual reward is obtained by demoralising fellow human beings.
2 The inclination to be anxious about circumstances that cannot be altered or put right.
3 Asserting that a thing will not happen because we cannot make it happen.
4 Not letting go of minor obstructions and problems.

5 Avoiding growth and enhancement of the mind, body and spirit.
6 Showing no curiosity in enquiry, learning, reading and discussion.
7 Trying to force other people, through your thoughts and actions, to believe and live as you do.

Be aware of these pollutions whenever they occur in your life and reject them by consciously refusing to follow them.

STEP 4 DEVELOP THE FOUR WISE ONES

The four wise ones are those pure thought energies that can most easily bring spiritual consciousness directly into our lives.

ACCOMPLISHMENT

Accomplishment is the use of thought energy to create events, situations and circumstances. It does this with natural ease because accomplishment knows how to attract the right thoughts, bringing them together to create positive, successful conclusions and outcomes.

POWER

Power comes from knowing how thought energies work together and from applying compassion and kindness to all expressions of thought energy. It is linked to the other three wise ones. By developing insight and acceptance and by accomplishing positive outcomes you create power for yourself. Power grows. As you achieve it, it will increase.

ACCEPTANCE

Acceptance is the understanding that comes from knowing

that in life there are some things we cannot change and that we must face these situations with patience and try to learn from them. Acceptance is a hard lesson to learn, but when we learn it a great and profound thought energy is then released into our daily lives and we experience contentment and beauty in everything we do.

INSIGHT

This thought energy shows us the true nature of any idea, energy, emotion, identity, person, event or situation, whether it be in the past, the present or the future. With insight you know how things were, why they are and what they will be. The past, present and future connect in one everlasting moment which lies within you, accessed by your consciousness. Insight brings knowledge of the flow of time, cause and effect. You will be able to see life.

All these thought energies can be made active in your life by asking them to become a part of your daily experience.

STEP 5 CONNECT WITH YOUR SOUL

The soul is light. Not the sharp flash of intellect or the burning flame of the will, but a light of pure thought energy that shines through us, clear and soft, waiting for us to recognise it. Soul thought energy desires a harmonised universe and this impulse is the drive towards human spirituality, enlightenment and the means to be happy, safe and secure.

Each of us is a unique combination of soul thought energy and we have within us something that, within the Bön tradition, is called the Great Inheritance. This is a simple, profound and natural state of mind that exists independently of all our other states of being. It is the essence of everything;

all our thoughts and life experiences stream out from it into the dimensions of mind and matter. From it come time, space, past and present and in recognising it we gain the ability to reach eternal comprehension.

THOUGHT EXERCISE FOR INVOKING YOUR SOUL

This is a traditional Tibetan Bön method of awakening profound knowledge within you that is beyond the intellect or the everyday mind. It is safe, enlightening and brings many rewards. Follow these six points of instruction below exactly and you will consciously experience the divine coming alive within you.

---

1 Sit comfortably. Close your eyes and let your breathing be even and normal. Focus upon your physical heart. Let your mind be absorbed into the beating of your physical heart. As this happens, start to feel moving streams of energy.

2 These streams of energy are flowing from your feet up through your legs, into your groin and towards your heart. Others flow through your hands, arms, lower back and spine and into your heart. More streams of energy flow into your throat then down into your heart. All the streams of energy throughout your body meet in your heart.

3 In the centre of the crown of your head, energy starts to move down to your forehead, along the bridge of your nose, inside the roof of your mouth, down through your tongue into your chest and then into your heart, meeting the other streams of energy there.

4 All the energy that flows to your heart gathers and slowly moves up through the centre of your body to the crown of your head, into the very centre, where it moves out of the centre of your head, flowing as a stream of pulsing, living, pure white energy.

5 This stream of energy gathers to the right side of you, forming itself into

a living pillar of luminous soul energy. At this point, acknowledge its presence and ask it in your own words to help you to reach a state of pure, spiritual consciousness.

6 When you have finished, mentally direct the soul energy back into the centre of the crown of your head where you may leave it until you need it again.

With the help of this pure soul energy you will be able to reach consciousness and thus to see that time is nothing more than the opportunity for you to discover the wisdom within your heart.

In understanding this you will see through your identity, the part of you that believes life is only about responding to the demands of your immediate environment. As it fades it will reveal the truth of who you really are. And as this happens, connections between the world and your inner life start to sprout and your consciousness develops, so that you will, increasingly, be able to connect with it with greater ease.

You will now understand that you are all things. You are creation in descent into matter and matter ascending into creation.

All things of this world and the universe coexist in your mind. You are the sum total of all humanity and each thought you have is a doorway to the pure thought energy that is in everything.

THE PATH OF SIMPLICITY

The Bön teachings state that the more hurriedly and desperately we search for happiness and meaning the faster we stir up a whirlwind of spiritual thought energy which will only lead to discontent, want and ignorance.

If we become softer and slow our rush, the fear of desperation will fall away and we can then hear the tender voice of pure thought energy wishing only to guide us.

Make things simple in your life. Let your life become simple in its actions, communicate simply and let your love be simple, for then it will be profound. Cultivate your integrity and inner balance and you will find your centre of pure thought energy. It will flow into your life, bringing you all that you need. In your own time you will come to see the simple truth, that the world is a perpetual wonder, created instant by instant by thought energies and that the universe is expressed in all our thoughts, in the spaces between moments and in the sparks of time.

When you recognise these truths and see the divinity in all things you can live free from anxiety and fear, with contentment and trust, safe in the knowledge that all is exactly as it should be.

The sky was overcast and grey as the lightning flashed through the clouds, arching to top of the mountain above me. The boom of thunder was deafening and I could smell the power of the storm in the air.

My teacher had died some months before and I was there in the sacred place, empowered by the ancient Bön tradition, upon Mount Pihanga. I had come to meditate and create my future.

I had also come, following my teacher's instructions, to give a blessing energy that he had made years before and allowed to grow in power to the Maori tribes who allowed my teacher to use their sacred mountain.

The tribes, Ngati Turangitukua and the Ngati Tuwharetoa, were blessed.

The teaching had now come full circle.

The lightning was travelling down the side of the mountain towards me when my teacher appeared to me.

'Lightning is the thought energy of ancient divinity.'

'It is electricity,' I replied.

'Electricity is the thought energy of ancient divinity.'

I smiled.

'Everything is thought energy,' he said.

Suddenly a bolt of lightning hit the spot where my teacher stood; it started to writhe and spiral as if it were a waterfall, but one waterfall that was sky-bound.

'Do you want to come with me?' he said.

'No,' I said, 'my journey is here.'

He stood there within the lightning, then smiled and was gone.

I packed my bag and began the long walk down. As I reached the tree line and entered the native forest of tall rimu trees, I turned back to pay my respects for the final time. Wind fluttered through the trees, and in the rustling of the leaves I heard the voice of my teacher and the voices of the ancient line of teachers softly speaking these words to me: 'Thought energy comes from the chaos that exists within all living creatures, all aspects of this world and the universe. Some chaos is good, some indifferent, some bad; however, it is the stuff from which happiness and enlightenment are made.'

Thunder rolled across the mountain. Rain fell to wash everything away.

'A new start,' said the rain.

'A new mind,' said the wind.

'A new me,' I said aloud.

Out from the mountain I walked, carrying a new way of thinking.

If you would like to know more about the work of Christopher Hansard or The Eden Medical Centre, please contact:

Katharine Parry
Practice Manager
Eden Medical Centre
63a Kings Road
London
SW3 4NT
United Kingdom

++44 (0) 2078815800
email: krp@edenmedicalcentre.com
website: www.edenmedicalcentre.com

The Bön Foundation
PO Box 826
Exeter
NH 03833–0826
USA
Tel: (603) 778–6997
Fax: (603) 778–1823

Email: *info@bonfoundation.org*
www.bonfoundation.org

INDEX